T0129180

THE
Motherhood
DIARIES

Also by ReShonda Tate Billingsley
Help! I've Turned Into My Mother

THE Motherhood DIARIES

ReShonda Tate Billingsley

STREBOR BOOKS

NEW YORK LONDON TORONTO SYDNEY

Strebor Books
P.O. Box 6505
Largo, MD 20792
http://www.streborbooks.com

© 2013 by ReShonda Tate Billingsley

ISBN 978-1-59309-499-7
ISBN 978-1-4767-1145-4 (ebook)
LCCN 2012951354

First Strebor Books trade paperback edition April 2013

Cover design: www.mariondesigns.com
Cover photograph: © Keith Saunders/Marion Designs

10 9 8 7 6 5 4 3 2 1

Manufactured in the United States of America

For information regarding special discounts for bulk purchases, please contact Simon & Schuster Special Sales at 1-866-506-1949 or business@simonandschuster.com

The Simon & Schuster Speakers Bureau can bring authors to your live event. For more information or to book an event, contact the Simon & Schuster Speakers Bureau at 1-866-248-3049 or visit our website at www.simonspeakers.com.

For my children…who keep me young and make me old

contents

Introduction

Ever since I was a little girl, I've kept a diary. I've always loved putting my innermost thoughts on paper. Granted, the older I got, the longer and longer the time between entries, but you could always count on me to write my feelings down.

Couple that love of writing with the fact that I can be somewhat of a pack rat, and a good cleaning of the closet can produce some amazing things—like all my stuff from high school: my yearbook, memory book, report cards, awards, certificates, and, yes, my teenage diary.

After one afternoon of spring cleaning, I started re-reading my diary, which I'd kept throughout high school. Seeing some of the absolutely hilarious and unbelievable things I wrote had my mouth open in amazement.

After my entertaining read, I tossed the diary back in the box and returned to my new forum for sharing my thoughts—social media. Instead of writing out all the shenanigans of my life on paper, I shared them with 5,000 of my closest friends on Facebook (yeah, I know, I'm addicted to social media). I did reserve *some* stuff for my journal, but for the most part, everything in my life was fair game.

On social media, I got immediate reaction from my updates on my never-a-dull-minute life. On a daily basis, someone was saying, "You and your family should have a reality show." (Not going to happen because while the kids and I don't mind the limelight, my husband isn't feeling it.) Or, one of my status updates on something one of my kids did would easily and quickly get hundreds of likes, re-shares, and re-tweets.

It was while reading some encouraging words on Facebook and Twitter that I came up with the idea for this book. I've actually started each chapter with an entry from my childhood diary, or from my "Mother Journal" (Yes, I graduated from a "diary" to a "journal.")

By no means do I purport to be some kind of therapist, child psychologist, parental expert, or anything of the like. I'm just a mother who has been there, done that, and has the war bruises to prove it.

As the mother of three ~~spoiled~~ wonderful, precious ~~tyrants~~ children, ages thirteen, ten and five, I think I've got this motherhood thing down (hey, I said I've got it down, I never said I mastered it), so I have some stuff worth sharing.

Now, before I go any further, let me give my disclaimer. I love my kids. I will always love my kids; they are the joy of my life. Keep that in mind as you read the rest of the book. Know that underneath it all—the sarcasm, the humor and the rants—I love my babies. On my good days and my bad days. On days that I have to keep reminding myself that I don't look good in orange jumpsuits with numbers on the back. On days when I act like I'm suffering from an extreme case of Tourette's. Even on those days, I love my children.

My kids also only know the sweet, loving mom (with an occasional side of crazy). So, don't worry, I am not, nor will I ever be, one of those "I wish you were never born" mothers. The damage from that could be irreparable. And I know one day they'll read this book (the oldest already read it and tried to add her own two cents.) But they know no matter what, at the end of the day, Mommy loves them.

Now that I have that out of the way...sometimes I have thoughts that maybe I should've pulled instead of pushed (okay, so I had a C-section, but you get my point.) Sometimes I lock the door to my kids' own personal World War III and ask myself, is *THIS* what I signed up for??? Sometimes I sit in my car in the driveway just because I don't want to go inside! And sometimes, I hide in the closet just so I can enjoy a pack of M&M's without having to share them.

While you're reading, I feel compelled to remind you that this is a lighthearted read. I hope that you'll get something within the pages, even if it's nothing but some laughter. But hopefully, you'll see someone you know, or yourself for that matter, and maybe, just maybe, you'll understand that you're not in this battle alone.

But whatever you do, don't call Child Protective Services on me. Don't write me hate-filled letters about how I should recognize that my children are angels, gifts from God, and I should cherish them every single day. Yeah, yeah, yeah. I know all that. But this ain't that kind of book.

The Motherhood Diaries is all about exploring the good, the bad, and the ugly side of my motherhood path and the paths of women who walk a similar Calgon-take-me-away journey on a daily basis. It's for women who love their children, but occasionally say, *What the hell was I thinking?* It's for women who complain, fuss, and rant about their kids but will go Mama Tiger crazy if you mess with one of their babies. It's for women, who no matter what, wouldn't trade their children for anything in the world (even if sometimes they want to drop them off at the nearest fire station— to avoid arrest—and speed off).

Tackling topics such as (not) having it all, the crazy things kids say, and mothering in the New Millennium, *The Motherhood Diaries* covers the things many mothers think about but are afraid to admit. And make sure you check out the Motherhood Stories from other writers at the end of the book. Some are funny. Some are serious. All of them are touching.

Motherhood requires a sense of humor—even if you just have to laugh to keep from crying. I hope you'll maintain one throughout this book. Personally, I'm not expecting to win any "Mother of the Year" awards with my parental skills, but I have no doubt that I'll be just fine when it comes to raising my kids. And I hope that someone, somewhere will read something that resonates with them and recognize we're all in this together!

Enjoy,
ReShonda

Be Careful What You Wish For...

Sept. 1, 1999

Dear Diary,

It has been four days since I found out I was pregnant and I am still absolutely overjoyed! I'm anxious, scared (not to mention broke from buying all the baby books out there). I have no doubt I'll be a good mother. This baby is a dream come true. Suddenly, nothing in life (including my career, which I was once so into) seems important. I wanted to be the next Oprah (she's the hottest talk show host in the country.) Now, I just want to be the best mother possible. All that matters is making my baby's life in the womb, the safest it can be for his or her glorious entry. I'm sooooo happy.

Nov. 7, 2001

Dear Diary,

Well, it looks like Mya is about to get a little sister. Found out I was pregnant again a few months ago. I was a little stunned at first, but I'm getting excited because the girls will be close in age. I hope they'll be the best of friends. I haven't been keeping up with my entries like I wanted. Being a Super Mom is hard :-). It looks like I'm about to give this motherhood thing another try.

Oct. 3, 2006

Dear Diary,

Oh, my God! I'm pregnant again. I think I need a drink.

These are actual entries from my journal. I am amazed at my range of emotions with each pregnancy. Don't get me wrong, I love all my kids equally, but the joy at news of their conception elicited a different reaction each time.

Let me start with my first born. After three years of marriage, my husband and I decided it was time to bring a life into this world to share in our blissful joy. But after spending all my life trying NOT to get pregnant, getting pregnant would prove easier said than done.

We tried everything—ovulation predictors, calendar counting, folic acid, standing on my head after sex, then eventually, fertility treatments. After the emotional roller coaster of a miscarriage, I finally got the news that I'd prayed for, cried for, and dreamed of. I was pregnant again.

Once I made it through the first trimester, I got over my fear of miscarrying again. I prepared to bring my baby into the world. I read every parenting book, subscribed to every email (I still get those freaking emails from Babycenter.com and my kid is thirteen years old.) I wanted to be the perfect mom. I had my super-hero cape nicely starched. I took pictures of my growing belly. I bought that little device that let me listen to my child's heartbeat and I fell asleep each night listening to the soft thump of her heart. I hired a young artist to hand-paint decorations on her wall. I decorated her room with the best furniture and I bought her the cutest little designer clothes. Nothing was too good for my little princess.

Since she was to be the first grandchild, my family was also eager for her entrance. My mother and sister had flown up to Oklahoma City, where I was living at the time, to be with me as I brought this bundle of joy into the world.

And boy, was I ready to bring her! I had done the Lamaze

classes and read more books than the downtown library could hold. I was educated to the point that I could teach some pregnancy classes myself, and when the doctor suggested a C-section, I balked in horror. I was a "real woman." My baby was coming in only one way—through the birth canal.

Or at least that's what I thought until I went into labor and was told the umbilical cord was wrapped around her neck and we needed to do an emergency C-section right away. At that point, any foolish perception about what made a real woman went out the window. Only one thing mattered—my baby's safety.

Four hours later, the nurses placed my tiny baby girl—Mya—on my chest. My husband stroked my hair. "She's so beautiful," he said, pulling the blanket back, so I could get a good look.

I smiled as I glanced at her, then frowned in horror. "Oh, my God; what's wrong with her?"

The nurse laughed. "She's just bruised. Really bad."

That was the understatement of the year. This child looked like she'd just gotten out the ring with Muhammad Ali, Joe Frazier AND Mike Tyson.

"But…but," I stammered. How could I voice what I was thinking? How could I tell my family, the doctors, anyone, what I was really thinking, which was *What is that thing?* What was I supposed to do with this little caramel thing with red pock marks all over her body? And to top it off, she was bald-headed!!! Like, not a lick of hair anywhere. Like, you couldn't tell which was smoother, her head or her butt. I had bought baskets of pretty little bows. What was I supposed to do with those now???

"Shhh, don't cry," my husband said with a huge smile. Men can be so clueless. He thought my tears were because of the beauty of giving birth, and I was crying because I was trying to think of ways I was going to hide my child from the world.

And then she smiled.

My baby smiled, displaying the biggest dimples I'd ever seen and my heart melted. And I reminded myself that she'd just had five feet of umbilical cord trying to strangle her to death. Of course she was bruised! And her hair? Well, I would just have to learn to get creative with hats and scarves, which is exactly what I did. My child had a hat or a scarf to go with every single outfit to cover the fact that her hair didn't start growing until she was four years old.

I chronicled my emotional journey each day, beginning a diary to my daughter that I planned to present to her on her eighteenth birthday.

I documented everything. Starting with my pregnancy, throughout her birth, her first steps, her first smile. You name it, I wrote it down. I have the ultrasound picture, the first doctor's report—even the pregnancy stick.

Two years later, enter baby number two. I guess the thrill had diminished some because her journey wasn't documented as well and I definitely didn't keep any of her *six* pregnancy sticks. (Yes, six. I had to be sure!) Her birth was drama-free (but don't tell her because I'll lose my leverage). I scheduled a C-section, showed up at the appointed time, and *voilà!* Baby! (My husband says my first words when she came out were, "Does she have hair?" But I'm gonna blame that one on the drugs; at least that's my story.)

My second child, whom I named Morgan, always jokes that getting her sister's hand-me-downs began when she was in the womb. I can't argue with that, because she's right. I used the same heart monitor to listen to her heart. I used the same breast pump, the same maternity clothes, the same cute baby clothes (but to my credit, Mya had so many clothes that she didn't get to wear, that many of them were still brand-new.)

What I didn't duplicate was the journal. I wanted Morgan to have her own. I started the same concept with her and got as far as...buying the journal. (Actually, I did write in it—twice.) I had good intentions, but the reality of motherhood set in.

By baby number three, five years later, I think I wrote my emotions on the back of a Subway napkin. And since that was a surprise pregnancy, well, let's just say, I'm going to leave it at that. (Eventually, my son will learn to read and I'd hate to have to spend thousands of dollars on therapy as he tries to come to terms with "how Mommy really felt.")

The bottom line is, I started off with good intentions with all my children and that's all that matters, right?

I think that's what happens to us all. We start off with grandiose intentions. We have all of these plans; then reality sets in. We quickly learn that motherhood isn't for the weak and that it takes a special kind of woman to navigate those choppy children waters. But we learn to do the best we can, and if we're lucky, the good times far outweigh the bad. And at the end of the day, that's all that really matters.

Motherhood Evolution

Dear Diary,

My mother came to visit this week. She fed my six-month-old collard greens and cornbread. She won't listen to anything I tell her about additives, insecticides, and new studies. Her response every time I complain is, "I don't need a damn book to tell me how to parent. I raised two children who turned out just fine."

I love my mom to death, but I can't wait for her to leave.

I was what you call a nervous mother. I was so scared of making the wrong choice, doing something out of order (at least for the first child). She got the entire house baby-proofed, from the corner edges to the drawer locks to the outlet plugs. By kid three, I was like, "Oh, a little electricity never hurt anybody."

It's not that I loved my kids any less, but I guess after the first child, that gene that makes you think motherhood is some blissful, beautiful thing slowly begins to evaporate. You realize that there's some validity to the three-second rule (if food drops on the floor and you pick it up within three seconds, it's safe to feed your kids. Hey, I don't make the rules!) And you also realize that no kid actually ever died from crying.

With my firstborn, I dropped her off at the babysitter, and came on my lunch break to nurse her, cuddle with her and *ooh* and *ahh* all over her. Everyone who kept her had to be thoroughly vetted like they were up for the Vice-Presidential nomination.

I was a little more lax on kid two. "Just make sure you don't kill her," was the extent of my instructions to the babysitter. And by kid three, I was putting an ad in the paper *Wanted: Someone to keep my kid!* (Not really, but it did feel like that from time to time).

By the birth of my son, that whole racing to pick up my kids was completely out the window and I began to cherish every solitary moment.

In fact, this conversation became a regular occurrence: My cell would ring. I'd answer with an agitated, "Hello."

"Hi, Mrs. Billingsley. It's Lisa from the daycare. Umm, are you coming to get Myles?"

Me, huffing and rolling my eyes. "Yeah, I have 'til 6:30. It's 6:29."

I tried to get it together, though, when at four, my son said, "Mom, why am I always the last kid at school?"

What I did find is that suddenly, things that came so easily for kid number one, became harder for number two and a downright struggle by three. Of course, in my idyllic world, motherhood was going to be a breeze. I know it hadn't been for my mother, but I was different. I was going to read up, be prepared and have the right mentality!

After Mya was born, I knew that I didn't want an only child. So after having one, I was like, "She needs a playmate." After two, I said, "Okay, I'm good."

The problem was we had two girls and my husband wanted a boy. By the third go-round, I said, "If you don't get your boy, you're just out of luck."

My girlfriend, Tori, wasn't so lucky. She tried and tried and tried and tried. She couldn't fathom a fifth child, so she gave up after the fourth girl. I want to contribute to her stress fund just thinking about that!

For us, though, the third time was a charm and my husband got his boy. Unfortunately, I'm not the young, virile mother I used to be and my son, well, I have to admit, he has a different set of rules than his sisters did.

"Why does Myles get away with so much?" my oldest daughter asked me one time.

"Because he's four and I'm forty," I replied. I'm not ashamed to admit it. I'm tired. Too tired to run after a rambunctious little boy. As long as he's not burning down the house, or destroying things, I'm good. I just have to deal with the occasional heart stoppers. Like the time he came barreling down the stairs and in a panic shouted, "Mommy, whatever you do, don't come upstairs," before turning and dashing back up the stairs.

Now, the part of me that was exhausted after running all day wanted to say "okay," and go back to watching Lifetime, but the rational part of me took over. I headed upstairs to find that he'd flooded the bathroom with his Transformer. (According to him, "Bumblebee had to take a dive in the toilet to escape the bad guys.")

A perusal of our family photo album also shows my evolution through my kids. The first fifteen pages are Mya in every form (first smile, first meal, sleeping, crying, playing). Then, there is a page-and-a-half of Morgan (who was the most adorable little thing), and since Myles was a boy, he got about ten pages.

I know, sad, right? (Insert the *Brady Bunch* line, "*Marsha, Marsha, Marsha,*" when Jan screams about her sister getting all the attention.) I didn't even realize how bad it was until we were all looking through the album one day.

"Awwww, is that me, Mama?" Morgan asked.

"No, baby. That's Mya."

"Oh, is that me?"

"No, that's Myles."

After repeating this scene several times, Morgan finally said, "Where am I?"

I almost told her the truth. *Your mom was just trifling, honey.* But staring at her big doe eyes, I could only say, "Sweetie, we lost all your baby pictures in a horrible fire. But don't worry, from now on, we're going to capture everything."

Okay, so that was trifling, too. But my baby was pacified and it put me on notice. Now, I snap pictures of her every chance I get. So she might not have baby photos, but she'll definitely have childhood pictures!

I used to feel bad about how lax I became with each child, but I learned that it was okay to cut myself some slack.

Sometimes, though, it took my children to help me put things back in perspective. In my house, Frosted Flakes, Fruit Loops, and Cap'n Crunch make regular appearances. That wasn't always the case. For Mya, I actually got up and cooked her little miniature sausages and pancakes. By Morgan, it was just a scrambled egg every now and then. And Myles, well, he became the cereal king. In fact, he arose one Saturday morning to find me cooking breakfast in the kitchen.

"What are you doing, Mommy?" he asked.

I flipped the pancake. "I'm making breakfast, baby."

My son stared at me. At the skillet. At the spatula in my hand. "Like at IHOP?"

Sure, I felt incredibly guilty, but I learned to stop beating myself up. My son was as healthy as my daughters. And he felt no less loved because Mommy gave him Frosted Flakes instead of pancakes.

At one time or another, most mothers will feel some type of guilt, but it's important to understand that perfect parenting is an oxymoron. There are no set rules and you will drop the ball. When you do, just pick it up and keep moving.

My daughter Morgan came to me one day, upset when I'd missed a Mother-Daughter Cupcakes and Coffee event at her school because my plane was delayed getting back into town. She didn't care that the plane was delayed because of a blizzard. All that mattered was that Mommy wasn't there. I believe in focusing on the positive. I apologized, but told her I was off working, putting the finishing touches on a movie based on one of my books.

"And how cool will it be when your friends see your mom's movie and you on the Red Carpet at the premiere."

"Red Carpet? Can I bring Emily?"

I nodded, even though I didn't know who the heck Emily was. Then I offered to come talk to her class about writing books and making movies and suddenly, Morgan was floating on Cloud Nine because her friends told her her "mom was super cool."

What I effectively did was acknowledge that I had missed her event, apologize, then find something positive to focus on. Kids really are resilient and they are accepting of our mistakes.

Guilt is a natural part of motherhood and comes from wanting to be a good mother to your children. However, in the end, it will weigh you down. If I can say I evolved in any way over the course of my three children, it was in learning to let go of the guilt. I woke up one day and realized my kids just loved "Mommy Time." It didn't matter if it was over a four-course meal or chili dogs. One thing I've finally learned from motherhood is that I should never feel guilty about taking care of me.

I ~~can~~ can't Have It All

Dear Diary,

I can't wait to grow up. I already have my life mapped out. In five years, I'll graduate from college—with honors. I'll meet and marry my college sweetheart in a big, lavish wedding. I'm going to have five kids and two dogs. I'll be an author, an anchor and an actress. Oh yeah, and I'm going to be the best mom in the whole world! I know that seems like a lot, but I don't care what anyone says. I know that I can have it all.

That is an actual entry from my diary, dated Sept. 9, 1986. It's quite hilarious now that I had my life mapped out so. And back then, you couldn't have told me that I wouldn't make it happen. But I do think I should get an "E" for Effort. I did graduate from college. (That whole honors thing? Yeah, maybe if my biology class wasn't the same time as *All My Children*, I would've never gotten a "D" and my GPA wouldn't have plummeted, and I could've graduated with honors. So I blame Agnes Nixon, the creator of *All My Children*, for that.)

Meet and marry my college sweetheart? For fear of getting sued, I'm not going to touch that one.

Five kids? (Insert hysterical laughter here.)

I did have two dogs, but they were demon dogs, so I gave them away to the first ~~unsuspecting~~ person that asked for them.

Five kids? (Yeah, I had to repeat that one.) Did I really think that I wanted five kids??? Don't get me wrong, I have nothing but respect for you mothers with your own basketball team. I thought that would be me. I come from a big family. My mom has eight brothers and sisters. My dad has seven. So it seemed quite natural that I would have five—until I had one.

How do you even manage that many kids in this day and age? A trip to McDonald's can easily run forty bucks. Not to mention, that's five soccer games, five mouths to feed, and if they're girls, five heads to comb.

I decided to ask my friend, Della, how she manages with her brood.

"How do you go out to eat with five kids?" I asked her.

"You don't," she replied.

Two simple words that had summed up her life.

Yep, I must've been out of mind to even think about five kids.

Authors Becky Beaupre Gillespie and Hollee Schwartz Temple say that a paradigm shift in motherhood is key to having it all. They argue that in this day and age, having it all simply means creating an "all" that you love.

In their book, *Good Enough is the New Perfect*, Gillespie and Temple say that more and more mothers are losing their "never enough" attitude and embracing a "good enough" mindset to be happier, more confident and more successful.

I knew I was on to something. What I'm giving is good enough for me.

I want my cake, and to eat it, too!

Early in my literary career, I pitched an idea for a book called *You Can Have it All.* My agent and editor passed on it, and at the time, I thought they had lost their minds. This was going to be a masterpiece about balancing motherhood with your career. It was going to explore how a woman could be Superwoman, wearing her pink cape for home, her red cape for work, her blue cape for community service and her yellow cape for "me" time. Yep, I had it all figured out. This was going to be a blockbuster and I was going to be a shining example of how a woman could have everything her heart desired.

That's why I was dumbfounded when my editor and agent didn't seem too interested. But maybe that's why they do what they do and I do what I do. Maybe they had the foresight to know that I was a naïve new mother who only *thought* she could have it all.

It took some adjusting and lots of missed soccer practices, late arrivals to work, and drive-thru dinners for me to realize that I *couldn't* have it all. Oh, I could try. I could try to work my full-time demanding job as I climbed the corporate ladder, raise three well-rounded, healthy children who participated in extracurricular activities and excelled in academics. I could have all of that. All I needed to do was open up my computer screen and create that fictional story. Because that's what that is—fiction. Sure, there are some mothers who defy the odds and do well at balancing, and on some days, I'm that mother. On most days, I'm not.

The realization that I couldn't have it all came in one of the most embarrassing moments of my professional career. I was a television news reporter in Oklahoma. I was out on assignment when we were sent to the scene of some breaking news.

In those situations, there's no time to do much of anything. You rush on to the scene, jump out and begin going live. This particular day, I did just that, giving all the information about the bank robber and what had happened. Throughout the taping, my photographer had a horrible look on his face. I had no clue what was going on. Maybe the job was stressing him out. Maybe he was worried that we weren't going to get the details of the robbery correct. But things were moving too fast for me to get to the root of his issue.

Finally, after wrapping the story and sending it back to the anchors in the newsroom, I looked at him. "Hey, what's wrong with you?"

"Ah, ah, um m," he stuttered.

"What is going on?" Now I was about to get worried because he looked mortified.

Then, without saying a word, he slowly pointed at my chest. "What?" I replied, glancing down at my emerald green silk blouse and the two round wet spots at my nipples. That's right, I had leaked right through my breast pads and on to national TV.

"Why didn't you say something?!" I screamed.

"Say what? You're the one talking about being supermom. I thought you would be prepared for anything."

"I was prepared. I had on breast pads," I cried, now covering my chest.

He grimaced like that was too much information, and started packing his gear, a sign to me that he had no interest in continuing this conversation. All I could do was get into the truck and burst into tears.

Yes, my leaking nipples were the talk of the newsroom, the talk of the town for that matter. (I thank God there was no YouTube back then.)

"You don't need to be breastfeeding that two-year-old anyway," my mom said when I later shared my disastrous story with her.

I took offense to that. Number one, my daughter was eighteen months; and number two, yes, I knew my daughter was breast-feeding even though she was potty trained (something else my mother had a major issue with), but I was being supermom, providing my daughter with a healthy foundation, all the natural nutrients I could give. (I only made it to six months of breast-feeding on Baby #2, and three on Baby #3.) Besides, I'd worked too hard to get her to latch on (the horror stories of my breast-feeding adventures would make up a whole other book.)

I think it was then that I realized that having it all was hard. I'm trying to report the news with pulsating boobs, sneaking into the bathroom at work to pump, going on business trips and literally crying as I had to pump, then pour my breast milk down the sink (any lactating woman knows breast milk is a precious commodity.)

I travel a lot as an author and on one visit to California, a male reader told me, "You're away from your kids a lot."

"Yes," I replied.

"You couldn't be my wife," he said, shaking his head in disgust.

I stared at him for a moment. "Good thing I'm not your wife."

But I did realize that he was on to something. Up until that point, I thought I was supermom. But a supermom would've been at home, catering to her children's every need. At every activity, doing homework every night, reading bedtime stories, etc. And since I've never been the stay-at-home type, I needed to find my "good enough." Which is exactly what I did. Yes, I continued to travel for work, but I got in, got out and returned home to my family. For me, that allowed me to enjoy my life and my kids.

I also quickly learned a true supermom knew how to ask for help, and that I did, from the maid to the babysitter. It's not like I was rolling in dough, but I finally had to say, I can spend six hours cleaning, then be too exhausted to enjoy my family, or I can spend those six hours working to make money to pay someone to clean, and come home to a clean house and my family will get a happy, rested mommy.

I now know that it's okay to not have it all. And as long as it's good enough for you, it's good enough.

Kids Say (and Do) the Darndest Things!

Dear Diary,

My four-year-old needs a muzzle. I'm shocked that I'm saying that about a four-year-old, but there's no nice way to put it. If he thinks it, he will say it. Today, he asked an overweight relative if she was expecting a boy or a girl. She replied, "What? Why do you think I'm pregnant?" He calmly answered, "I don't really. But it would've been really rude to call you fat." I wanted to laugh and hang my head in shame at the same time. Thank God she has a sense of humor.

That incident was one of many that has had me hanging my head in shame when it comes to my children. When I was crafting my life plan, nowhere did I say, "Lord, send me three hilarious children who keep me on my toes with their shenanigans." But I have to admit, they keep me laughing. (I'd love to say that laughter keeps me young, but the way my knees are hurting right now, that theory is out the window.)

Each day is a new experience with my kids. I never know what's in store. Take one day when my son was four, for example. He came running into my room with his eyes squeezed tightly closed.

"Help! Help!" he screamed as he frantically fanned his eyes.

"Oh, my God," I said in a sheer panic as I wiped his eyes. "What happened, baby?"

"I peed in my eyes!"

Blank stare.

Seriously? How is that even humanly possible? I'd changed enough diapers to know what he was working with. In the face? *Really?*

That ended up being one of those things I never figured out and eventually stopped trying. And, of course, my husband was no help. He just stood in the back with his chest out, talking about "That's my boy."

Now, we're proud of our son peeing in his face? Men!

Despite all the stories I share, I'm not one of those moms who wants to tout every spectacular thing her child has ever done, or who wants to whip out the portfolio of all her kids at various stages, but my kids are pretty darn funny.

Sometimes, it's to the point that you have to turn your head and laugh because you don't want to cosign what they're saying or doing, which is often over the top.

My son—who is the funniest of them all—attended his sister's school play last year. She was so excited about the play and was extremely proud of her role. She'd practiced for weeks and urged us to be on time so we could see her debut.

We arrived early and took our seats in the auditorium that was quickly filling up. I was snapping pictures; my oldest was texting her friends and completely not interested; and my son—well, he was pouting because I had to pull him away from his favorite TV show, *The Power Rangers.*

Finally, after twenty minutes, the moment we had all been waiting for arrived. Morgan took the stage, held her head up high and said, "I am a lion, hear me roar!" Then she stepped back and took her place in line.

My son looked at me in horror, then loudly said, "Are you kidding me? That's it? I missed *Power Rangers* for *that*???"

This is the same kid who declared in the Disney Store that we should get his Incredible Hulk mask from there and not from

Walmart, where I was sure it was twenty bucks cheaper because "Disney was the real deal and Walmart was just a bootleg version of Disney." The same kid who begged for a "Baby T" necklace so he "can be cool." Don't know what a "Baby T" necklace is? Neither did I until my son said, "You know, Mom, like for Jesus."

"You mean a cross?" I asked.

"Yeah, like I said, Baby T."

And yet another conversation:

"Mom, can I watch cartoons?"

"No, Son, you have to do your homework," I replied.

"My homework is coloring. Why don't I just point out the color of the *Power Rangers*?"

Long sigh. "No, that's not gonna work."

"Is there a book that says parents have to take all the fun out of everything?" he huffed.

"Boy, go do your homework."

He was grumbling as he walked off. "Man, kindergarten is sucking the life out of me..."

Then there was the time I walked in on him praying.

"Dear God, please make my mommy really fat."

Now, normally, I wouldn't interrupt a prayer, but that required immediate action.

"Hey, hey, Son. Why would you say something like that?"

"Because I really want a little brother," he replied matter-of-factly.

Umm, yeah, God, are you listening? That's a prayer we definitely DON'T want answered!

His older sisters have their own individual senses of humor. Morgan's is a dry humor—the kind that makes her funny without even trying.

Like when we were all sitting around my mom's dining room

table finishing up Sunday dinner. My mother, sister and I were reminiscing about my grandmother, who was affectionately known as Madea (it's a Southern thing).

"You know, Madea has been dead twenty-five years today," my mom said.

Morgan, who never bothered to look up from her Nintendo DS, said, "So, how does she keep making movies?"

It took a moment for all of us to register that comment, and then we burst out in laughter when we realized she thought we were talking about Tyler Perry's Madea character. Needless to say, my mom admonished my lack of giving my children family history lessons.

People tell me all the time that I'm pretty funny. I don't see it, but maybe that's because it's just a part of who I am. And I guess that's who my kids will be, too.

But that's okay because nothing brings a family together like a little laughter.

They've Been Here Before

Dear Diary,

I like Michael Jackson's music, but not to the point that I play it on a regular basis, or even talk about him or his music. So, why then, is my son obsessed with the deceased singer? How can he possibly be so enamored with a singer he's only seen on YouTube? And that's not all. Today, he walked up, hit his sister, and started singing, "You just got hit by...a Smooth Criminal, *so* Beat It *before I call* Billie Jean *to go* Thriller *on you." How can a five-year-old know this stuff??????*

My grandmother used to say a child who was smart had "been here before" or was an "old soul." My children are definitely old souls who have been here before.

When my daughter, Mya, took off her diapers at thirteen months and declared that she was a "big girl" and wanted to wear "big girl panties" (yes, that was the extent of our potty training.) I was like, wow, she's pretty advanced. When Morgan pulled her own tooth because she was trying to get money for the new Barbie (I had no idea that's what she was planning when she asked me what was the going rate for the Tooth Fairy), and when Myles learned how to unlock my iPad (when even the man in the Apple store couldn't help me), I knew for a fact my children had been here before. I don't know that I really believe in reincarnation, but they do things that no child should know how do. Especially my son, who says and does things I'm convinced no three-, four- or five-year-old could know.

For example, when he was four, I awoke at six in the morning to him trying to put his sheet, nightclothes, underwear and blanket into the washing machine. He didn't have the first clue what he was doing, but that didn't stop him from desperately trying.

"Myles, did you pee in the bed?" I finally asked after watching him from the laundry room entrance for a few minutes.

"No, Mommy. It rained in my room last night." He actually said that with a straight face.

"So, it rained, inside the house, but the only thing that got wet was your bed and your clothes?"

He nodded like I was really going to believe that. And as usual, it took my stern mommy voice before he finally fessed up.

By age five, Myles had also learned the art of conning.

"Mommy, can I have five cookies?" he asked me in the kitchen one day.

I glanced up from the dinner I was preparing. "No, honey, you'll ruin your appetite."

"Please, can I have five. I'm really hungry." Insert pouty face, turn sideways so deep dimples can show, then bat eyes.

Long sigh. "No, but you can have *two* cookies."

A wide smile spread across his face. "Thanks, Mommy," he said as he bounced off to the pantry to retrieve his cookies.

A few minutes later, I walked in and overheard this conversation with his sister, Morgan.

"So, how did you get the cookies?" she asked in a hushed tone.

He smiled proudly. "I asked for five. That's what you gotta do. If you want three cookies, you gotta ask for six. That way they feel like they're making some kind of deal with you, but you got what you wanted in the first place."

I swear if I could've reached down his throat and retrieved those Oreos, I would have!

Another prime example of their "old souls" came when my daughter was hospitalized for pneumonia. First of all, she had to be the most difficult patient ever. Every time they tried to put an IV in, she screamed like they were giving her brain surgery with no pain medication. It literally took five nurses to hold her down. That part I can give her; needles scare everyone. But, at one point, the nurse dropped the needle on the floor, then picked it up. Before I could say anything, Mya sat up in the bed and said, "I know you're not going to use that dirty needle on me."

The nurse looked a little shocked. I could see she was wondering how my daughter knew that. I wanted to tell her, just like she knew everything else. She's been here before.

That was the only thing that I could tell my minister, who showed up with some deacons from our church to offer prayers for Mya in the hospital. As soon as the five men entered the room in their crisp, button-down suits, my daughter said, "Oh, my God. Are you guys from the government?"

They all looked at me in shock. But they didn't understand that I was just as shocked. I'd never been visited by anyone from the government. By the looks on their faces, you could see their minds churning. They probably were wondering if it was the FBI, Child Welfare, or Social Services that my daughter knew so well.

"I, I don't know where she got that from," I finally stammered. The minister flashed me a silent smile, but I know what he was thinking. *If you had your daughter in church more often, she would know I'm your pastor.*

There have been some proud mommy moments—at least temporarily. Like one Sunday morning when my son woke me up and said, "Mommy, come on. I really want to go to church."

I leapt from the bed, my heart euphoric. I was raising a good, Christian boy. A little boy who rose early Sunday morning and encouraged his family to go to church. It wasn't until we were pulling into the church parking lot and he said, "Hey, where are we going?" that I knew something was up.

"To church, Son," I replied. "Like you wanted."

He looked horrified. "But, umm, aren't we going to stop at the doughnut shop?" We often stopped there before church.

"No, Sweetie, we're late. I'm getting you to church."

"Aww, man." He pouted. "The only reason I wanted to go to church was because I wanted to go to the doughnut shop."

She now we have to get Doughnuts for Jesus? I was so not feeling that picture.

If my kids were here in a previous life, they were definitely "indoor" creatures. Growing up, my friends and I loved playing outside. Not these children. We recently took my kids to the country (my husband and I are both from Arkansas), where my husband's grandmother only gets one channel on her television. We took the kids' video games and told them to go outside and play.

"What are we supposed to do outside?" Mya asked.

"Go play in the streets like I used to do when I was little," I answered.

"There are bugs out there," Mya replied.

"That's dangerous," Morgan added.

"What if we get kidnapped?" Myles threw in.

It was the same type of reaction on a visit to Animal Kingdom, you know the place every kid dreams of going. After less than thirty minutes, they were ready to go.

"It's too hot, can we go?" Mya said.

"I'm itching, bugs are out here. Why can't we go?" Morgan added.

"Can we please go inside with the air conditioning?" Myles whined.

I looked at each of them. "No, you have three hundred thirty-six dollars' worth of fun that you're going to have, so let's get moving!"

I thought about what I wanted to be in my next life. After the day I had today (Mya broke her fourth pair of glasses, Morgan is distraught because she didn't get invited to a classmate's party, and Myles drew on my living room sofa with a Sharpie because he "was exercising his freedom of speech"—yes, that was his reply), part of me wants to say in my next life I want to be childless.

And then they smile. Or laugh. Or just hug me. And remind me that for all my gripes, I wouldn't change a thing!

Don't Judge Me...

Dear Diary,

Today, I saw a woman in Walmart who had parked her basket in front of a television in the electronics department and left it there. Oh, did I mention her toddler was sitting in it? Some of the shoppers were horrified. But I felt compelled to walk up to the lady and tell her, "I feel your pain."

I was recently shopping for a new car and I found myself walking around the parking lot, going, "If I didn't have any kids, I would get this." "Man, back when I didn't have kids, I would've gotten that."

It was at that point that I realized that most of what I did in life was determined PK and AK—pre-kids and after-kids. That Jimmy Choo luggage that I wanted for $3,000? Can't really get that when I don't have college tuition saved. That girls' weekend in Vegas. Can't do that AK. Even a night on the town requires a carefully orchestrated plan of action.

PK, I used to listen to all the child-rearing experts who advised that I limit my child's television consumption. But the first time I couldn't get Mya to settle down, and Teletubbies could; they became my new best friends. To this day, I have a love-hate relationship with Barney. My kids are old enough now, but I will admit, I used the TV to babysit on many days. I tried to offset their television time by making sure I read to them, but I turned to the TV more than I ever imagined I would have. It's amazing how much house-cleaning you can get done while *Caliou* is on!

Another thing I let slide was my children's sleeping conditions. Morgan wanted to sleep anywhere but the bed—the pantry, the hallway, the bathroom. You could put her in the bed and she would get right back out. I drew the line at the dryer (yes, she did make her way into the dryer one night), but everything else was fair game. My husband was mortified that I was letting my child sleep on the floor, but in motherhood, you have to pick and choose your battles and that was one that wasn't worth fighting.

My friend, Jaimi, had her children's schedule mapped out— snack at 10, nap at 10:23, etc., and I would ask myself, "What is wrong with me?" But then, I realized motherhood isn't a competition. So what if my baby had a stain on her shirt? So what if she didn't take a nap today? It's not about who does things the best— best for one person may not be best for another.

It wasn't as easy getting that message across to my husband. My son is very big for his age. My daughters were cheering for a Little League team and the coach was salivating at the mouth at the idea of my son playing. I kept saying, "He may be big, but he's not ready." Of course, the coach didn't believe me. Until he was finally old enough to play. We started him with baseball. During the very first game, a player from the opposing team got the ball and came after my son as he was heading to second base. My son, who thought he was Derek Jeter and Usain Bolt rolled into one, began zigzagging across the field, dodging the player and yelling, "Nah, nah, nah-nah, you can't catch me."

No matter how much we yelled, he continued running and sticking out his tongue until the catcher gave up.

Another time, he hit the ball, ran to first base, second base, then went straight for home plate. Everyone screamed to him, "You can't do that!"

He yelled back, "I'm taking a shortcut."

Needless to say, my husband finally realized fatherhood isn't a competition, either.

LIFE LESSONS

I really do try to be honest with my children. And forthcoming. After all, that's what I urge them to strive for, honesty before everything else. But when you have kids like mine, sometimes you have to roll with the punches.

I posted a status asking my friends on social media if their kids keep their rooms cleaned on their own, without being fussed at or threatened. I wanted to live vicariously through those individuals, since it seems like all I do is fuss about a dirty room. There were several people who replied that they had perfect little angels who kept their rooms clean. But I took comfort in knowing that most parents were like me.

I'd tried it all—fussing, nagging and round-the-clock admonishments. And my children would keep the room clean for maybe a day. I came home one day to see my son feverishly working to clean his room. He was running around, Pledge in hand, dusting, vacuuming, etc. This was the same little boy who always found an excuse—his pinky finger hurt, his eyeball socket was coming out—anything to get out of cleaning up. So needless to say, I was in awe.

"How did you get him to clean his room?" I asked my oldest daughter.

She leaned in and whispered, "We told him President Obama was coming to visit."

"So you lied to him?"

My daughter gave me a look. "Is his room getting cleaned or is it not?"

"You know I don't like you lying," I said.

She sighed. "Okay, I'll go tell him the truth."

"Wait," I said, stopping her. "We'll tell him the truth, later."

She smiled knowingly and I felt guilty. But when I saw that sparkly room, I pushed that guilt aside. "President Obama is going to be so proud."

Thankfully, my kid has a short attention span, so we were able to put on his favorite movie and he forgot all about it. From time to time he still asks me and I say, "The President got tied up." (Yeah, I know, lying).

My mother always used to say there are some things you should never say out loud. I took that philosophy into motherhood. So, when my newborn threw up all over my new designer dress (and trust me, it's not often that I do designer), I sucked it in. When my middle child cut a plug out of her beautiful head of hair, I calmly explained how that wasn't nice because Mommy had worked so hard to grow her hair. Even when my son took my brand-new MAC lipstick and colored his poster (because he couldn't find the red crayon), I sucked it up. But after years of sucking it up, smiling and pretending "Oh, that's just what children do," I woke up one day and told myself that niceness could only go so far.

So when my daughter, Morgan, announced that she was upset and leaving because I wouldn't let her have her way, I simply replied, "Okay."

I probably should've tried to convince her why she needed to stay and appreciate all that she had. But I did to her, what my mother would've done to me—I helped her pack. (On second thought, if it were my mom, I wouldn't have had to pack. There would've been no taking anything that she'd bought.) But I'm a twenty-first-century mom, so I was going to help her pack.

So after she had all her belongings in a duffle bag, she calmly tossed her bag over her shoulder and left. And I let her go. Yes,

I was watching from the window. She actually got to the corner. Then, she paused, as if she needed to figure out where to go next. Then, God stepped in.

A big roar of thunder filled the sky and my little diva turned around and ran as fast as she could back home.

ONE DAY AT A TIME

I was happy to see my son starting kindergarten, not just because it put him one step closer to graduation, but he really was looking forward to it. One of the very first things they taught him? My phone number. And he uses it. One hundred and twenty-seven times a day. Any time I am away from him, he calls me. If I'm outside, he calls me. If I'm in the other room, he still calls me.

"Hi, ReShonda," he said one time, trying to disguise his little voice. "This is your friend, Pat."

"Hey, Pat. I'm going to have to call you back," I said, playing along.

"Wait, Mommy, it's me! Don't hang up."

What in his little five-year-old mind makes him think I don't know it's him?

His use of the phone was so nerve-wracking that at one point, I drafted this email to his teacher…*I understand the need to teach my five-year-old my telephone number. But really??? Between calling and disguising his voice as "the preacher man" (guess u didn't teach him about caller ID) and calling me 437 times today…it is no longer cute. Please stick to ABCs…*

I don't know that I can quite blame the kindergarten teacher, though. All of my kids call me. And call me, and call me, and call me. Until I answer. If I ignore fourteen times, they'll call fifteen. I've tried to say, "If I don't answer right away, I'll call you back as soon as I can."

Of course, that never works. So sometimes, I turn off my phone just so I can enjoy some peace and quiet. I say a small prayer that nothing bad happens, but I need a few moments of solitude on my way home.

But turning off the phone isn't the worst thing that I do. I'm going to confess some things to you...just don't judge me.

Sometimes I think things that no mother should think. Nothing that warrants real psychiatric help (or a visit from Child Protective Services). But unconventional nonetheless. These are my confessions:

Sometimes I take the long way home.

Sometimes I get in my car and just want to keep driving.

Sometimes I go out to eat—alone—enjoying my steak dinner; then I come home and fix my kids hot dogs.

Sometimes I look at my kids and say to myself, "Is this what I dreamed of???"

And I would NEVER, EVER, EVER pick a favorite child. But if you put an AK47 to my head and said, "Okay, you gotta choose a favorite," it would be the unplanned surprise, my little boy. As my oldest daughter would say, "Tell us something we don't know."

Twenty Questions

Dear Diary,
I know that children are inquisitive, but sometimes I would give anything if they would just shut up.

I love the game Twenty Questions—at least when I'm playing it with my friends and there's a bottle of tequila at the center of the table. But when you have three inquisitive kids, suddenly that game is no longer fun.

I think my children wake up every morning thinking of some question that they can ask me. Some of the questions are legitimate questions, like "Why is it dogs weren't born the dominant species?" (Yes, she said "dominant." That damn Animal Channel). Others make no sense, like, "Why doesn't Friday come before Thursday?"

Some of the questions that I get in a typical day:

"When it gets dark, does that mean God has turned out the lights?"

"If you were a turtle and I was a lizard, would we be able to understand each other?"

"Why is day called day and night called night?"

"Why can't I sleep during the day and play at night?"

"If Daddy wasn't my daddy, would I still be me?"

The perfect mother would nourish her child's inquisitive nature with each and every question, but there reaches a point when you wish the word "why" had never been invented.

There are the questions that catch you off-guard, like when my son came bursting into my room and said, "Mommy, why does Mya wear diapers?" (It was her time of the month.)

After I composed myself, I took a deep breath, leaned in and whispered, "Sometimes your sister pees on herself."

Yeah, I know, I should have sat him down and explained the birds and bees. But my response was so much easier. He shook his head, mumbled, "That's just sad," and walked out the room.

From time to time I do answer questions logically, simply because the real answer wasn't pretty. Like when my daughter asked, "Why are your boobs so flabby?"

I had to take a deep breath on that one, then I calmly gave her the scientific answer. "As women get older, gravity sets in." In actuality, what I wanted to say was, "Because my kids sucked the life out of me and all the air out my boobs!"

Yeah, I know that would be taking it a bit far. Breastfeeding is a beautiful thing, right? My children got all their necessary nutrients the way that God intended. Who cares if it was at the expense of my once-perky boobs?

That wasn't the only time I had to get innovative in my answers. Former Destiny's Child member, Kelly Rowland, has a very sexually suggestive song that they play on the radio. (I know, I should probably change the station when this song comes on, but there's only so much Disney XM Radio a grown woman can take.) The song is called "Motivation," and it's basically Kelly telling her lover how to make love to her, adding that "when he's done, she doesn't want to feel her legs."

"Mom, what does she mean she doesn't want to feel her legs?" my daughter, Morgan asked.

"It means that she's working out with a trainer, and she wants to make sure it's strenuous so that she can lose weight."

She bought that explanation and I breathed a sigh of relief. Well, until a few minutes later when the "Size matters" commercial came on, talking about why women "prefer their men to be bigger and wider."

There was no explaining that one to the two pre-teen girls giggling like it was the funniest thing on earth.

So back to Disney XM Radio I had to go.

I recently won an NAACP Image Award for Outstanding Literary Work—Fiction. It was a proud moment for me and my family, especially my oldest daughter—but not until she verified it for herself. When I told her that I had won, she had to go to the NAACP website to make certain (as if I go around making up awards).

But she took her obsession with the award to a whole new level, when, after the event, she went online to view the photos, then came to me with handwritten notes "on my performance." Now, mind you, I was in the literary awards category, the part they do before the actual show airs. So my category wasn't televised. Still, my daughter managed to dig deep into the Internet until she found some photos.

Her assessment? "While you looked pretty, your pose was off and you're going to have to practice more for the next time." Of course, she added that had she been there, she would've made sure I struck a "celebrity pose" and not an, and I quote, "author who's just happy-to-be-there pose."

The funny part was—I *was* just happy to be there.

Tequila for Breakfast

Dear Diary,
I never have been much of a drinker. In college, I was always the kid
who stayed sober, so I could make sure everyone got home safely. So, why
is it I've now turned into a lush? Oh yeah. I have kids.

I was joking when I wrote that entry—at least about the lush
part. But I do find that with motherhood, Moscato has become a
really dear friend. I hadn't even noticed that I'd begun "indulging"
a little more than usual until one morning my husband approached
me while I was sipping a margarita.

"Are you really having Tequila for breakfast?" he asked. It
wasn't until that point that I realized that something was wrong
with this picture. But to my defense, my day had started at seven
a.m.—after we overslept and the kids missed the bus—again. Then,
my oldest had a major meltdown because it was picture day and
she had a "massive crater zit" at the center of her forehead. In
actuality, it was one of the smallest pimples I'd ever seen, but
who wanted to argue with twelve-year-old hormones at seven in
the morning?

As I was fighting with my son over why he could not wear his
Toy Story cowboy boots and shorts for picture day, Morgan kept
pulling my arm, saying, "Mom, should I smile like this?" (as she
flashed a toothy grin), "Or like this?" (as she gave an "I'm ten but
trying to seem sexy" look).

"The first one," I said, turning back to my son. "Take those boots off now," I told him.

"Okay, thanks, Mom. I'm going to do the second smile."

Thankfully, I don't curse out little children, so I shook my head and continued my cowboy boot fight. After doing that and barely getting them to school on time, I returned home to find that the dog had gotten out and was roaming the neighborhood (of course, I had to go track her down). After that, I had to deal with the lawn man accidentally cutting my sprinkler system, then pretending he didn't understand English. Anyone of sound mind and body would want a drink. The difference between me and a true lush is that I don't always act upon the urge to drink. Besides, I never reach the point of being drunk. I just fall into a deep sleep—something that became a rarity with motherhood.

But as much as my children can be little angels, I admit, sometimes I search their heads for three sixes. (You know, like the mom did in the *Omen* movies). As a God-fearing woman, I know that I have God-fearing children, but sometimes, each of them has a point when they turn into a demon child and it really makes me wonder. Or maybe, that's some kind of test of faith. Lord knows I prayed for their health and well-being, for peace of mind, for the strength not to kill them. In fact, I've adopted a prayer I heard my mother say when it came to my twelve-year-old. It started off with the standard "Lord's Prayer" and ended with "...please deliver me from beating the mess out of this child." When I first heard it, I was appalled, but now, I feel her. Completely. (Before you gasp, let me clarify, we don't *really* beat our kids. It's a figure of speech, maybe a messed-up figure of speech, but one of those bad habits that's been passed down through the generations.)

CALGON, TAKE ME AWAY

My children love talking to me—especially when I'm using the restroom (what is it about mom peeing that makes you want to stand and hold a conversation?) If they're not bogarting their way into the bathroom, they wait until I'm on the phone, or otherwise occupied, before trying to hold a conversation or ask me a hundred questions.

One day I was on the phone trying to conduct business when Mya came racing into the room, her sister right behind her.

"Mom! Morgan said she hates me!"

"But you said it first."

"That's because you're always messing with my stuff!"

I inhaled deeply and covered the mouthpiece with my hand. "Girls, I'm on the phone."

"But she's always in my stuff," Mya cried like it was the end of the world.

"You wear my stuff, too!"

I shot them dagger looks, motioned to the phone, then returned to the conversation. "I'm sorry, ma'am. You were saying, you'd like me to have this project to you when?"

The woman continued rattling off the details and the fight escalated.

"You make me so sick!"

"You make me sicker!"

Then the oldest pushed the youngest, who fell and started screaming like she'd been pushed into a smoldering volcano. And I snapped.

"Didn't you hear me say I'm on the friggin' phone??? I'm sitting here trying to get this job and y'all acting a damn fool!!"

Of course, since I'd taken it there, they immediately got quiet. So I took another deep breath and prepared to unmute the phone and continue my call. The problem was, it was already unmuted and said businesswoman was sitting there in silence.

"Oh, my God," I whispered. The woman was going to think I was some kind of psycho ghetto mom. "I'm sorry. It—it's my kids."

"It's okay," she said sympathetically. "I have four kids of my own, so I feel your pain."

And boy do I have pain. If my kids aren't fighting, they're making my gray hair grow by leaps and bounds. And oftentimes, it's their personalities that cause me the most grief.

Take Morgan. As the middle child, she's always in search of attention, so she tends to be a bit of a brown-noser, always trying to suck up to teachers, family members, and anyone else who can pat her on the head and say, "Good girl." At the same time, she truly does have a servant's heart; she loves helping people and giving them things. The problem is those things usually don't belong to her! A recent phone call from her teacher was a prime example.

"Hi, Mrs. Billingsley. How are you?" her teacher said after I answered my phone.

"I'm fine," I replied hesitantly. No teacher ever calls for good stuff.

"Well, I just wanted to say thank you for the Beats by Dr. Dre headphones you gave me."

That stopped me in my tracks. If you know anything about these expensive headphones, you'll know they cost around $200 and are extremely popular. Why anyone other than a deejay would need $200 headphones is beyond me, but they were a gift from my husband and I actually liked them a lot. (I think it was because when you put them on, you could literally drown outside noise.)

"Excuse me?" I said. "What do you mean *gave you*?"

"Well, Morgan gave me some headphones today, but I really feel like I should pay you for them. How much do I owe?"

After I shook myself out of my daze, I managed to get all the details. Morgan was basically trying to impress her teacher and gave her MY $200 headphones. Most kids give apples and my kid wants to give the most expensive headphones on the market!

"Yeah, I'm sorry, but I'm going to need to come pick those up tomorrow," I told the teacher.

The teacher was a good sport and returned the headphones, but it took everything in my power to, well, I'll let your imagination take over from here.

This wasn't the first time Morgan had tried to buy her way at school. On another occasion, a teacher called and said, "Morgan said that you said you would help me write my book."

I never said any such thing. But I'm trying to bite my tongue. "Umm, she said what?"

"That you could help me write my book. She also brought me a set of your books. I really appreciate this because I know this would've run me quite a bit to have bought all of these."

Who are you telling? The calculator in my brain was already going into overdrive. Twenty-five books at fifteen dollars each. Plus $150 an hour for consulting equaled my child had lost her damn mind!

I don't even remember how I got out of that, but I did sit Morgan down and have a long talk with her when she got home. Obviously, that talk didn't take since a few months later was when I got the headphones call.

Not to be outdone, I got a call from my son's teacher one day, telling me he had brought his Michael Jackson *Thriller* book to school and was using it to scare the little girls, so she'd confiscated it. Now, he knew he wasn't supposed to take the book to school, but it "accidentally fell into his backpack." (How an 11-by-17 hardback accidentally falls into a zipped backpack is yet to be determined.) We had had the "do not lie" talk, so I was going to give him a chance to come clean.

"Hey, Son, go get that Michael Jackson book so I can take it to the hospital tonight to read to your grandmother," I said.

He stood in silence for a minute. I'm sure the little angel and devil sitting on each shoulder were battling it out.

The devil must've won, because he said, "Mama, that book is pretty scary. I'm sure the doctor doesn't allow those types of books at the hospital."

Guess he doesn't know teachers email parents these days, but I kept at it. "It'll make her feel better."

"That book is really long, too," he continued, a look of genuine concern on his face. "Granny doesn't have time to be listening to all that. Plus Michael Jackson died. She doesn't need to hear about people dying when she's in the hospital trying to get better."

"Go get the book, Son."

He stood and thought for a minute. "Okay, let me go find it."

I was stunned that he was actually going to carry on this charade. About thirty minutes later, I walked in to see his sisters tearing up the living room, looking for the book, while he sat on the sofa playing with his Nintendo DS.

"We don't see it, Myles," Morgan said.

"Keep looking. It's gotta be here somewhere," he nonchalantly replied.

I couldn't take it anymore! I called his little behind to the carpet, and he finally came clean. But all I could think was, *I have thirteen more years of this???*

That is something I find myself saying—a lot.

I talk to my kids all the time, about what they should and shouldn't do. Most of the time, they listen. And when they don't, you can always count on them to find some kind of loophole.

Prime example: I opened my DirecTV bill one day and was shocked to find over a hundred dollars in pay-per-view movie charges. When I saw the names of the movies—*The Avengers*, *The Dark Knight*, I immediately suspected my husband. But then I saw *Scooby Doo*, *Harry Potter*, *Lord of the Rings*, many of them ordered three and four times, and I knew the culprit was none other than my son.

"Myles!" I screamed, adding his middle and last name, a sign that he was definitely in trouble.

"Yes, Mommy," he said, running into my room. "What did I do?"

The fact that you know you did something speaks volumes.

"Did you order movies on TV?" I asked, waving the bill.

"Yes, Mommy."

Wait. I wasn't prepared for the truth. "Ummm, wh-why in the world would you do that?"

He shrugged. "I wanted to see them. You said it was okay."

"I said that? When?" I immediately got on the defensive, wondering if he'd picked up his sister's tricks of asking me stuff while I was asleep.

"Remember, I always come and ask you," he said. "I said, can I watch *Batman*? You said yes."

I did remember that conversation. And I wasn't asleep. "But I was talking about *Batman*, not *Dark Knight*! *Dark Knight* costs six dollars to watch."

"But *Batman* is *Dark Knight*," he said innocently. He looked at me like it wasn't his fault that I didn't know the difference.

"Good-bye, Myles," I said, shooing him out of my room because technically, he was right. Good thing I have an R-rated block on my TV. Who would've thought that I would need to have a you-don't-order-pay-per-view-movies talk with a five-year-old?

There were a lot of talks I should've had (but didn't think I needed to) with my five-year-old—including what constitutes a real emergency.

One day, I had just pulled into the driveway when the police pulled up behind me.

"May I help you?" I immediately asked as the two men got out of their car.

"Yeah, we got a 9-1-1 call here," the first officer replied.

My heart raced. Visions of my children in all kinds of disastrous situations popped into my head. The sitter had to be unconscious or something because quite surely she would've called and told me something was wrong. I raced inside the house, cops behind me, to find Myles standing in the middle of the floor, his lips poked out, his arms crossed angrily over his chest. Mya was standing over him wagging her finger.

"Yeah, someone called 9-1-1?" officer number one asked. "Is everything okay?"

"No, it's not!" Myles barked. "I called you." Just from the pouty look on his face, I knew this conversation was not about to end well.

"What's the emergency, Son?" the officer asked.

"Mya won't let me watch *Power Rangers*."

Someone just dig me a grave and bury me now.

Both officers shot me a look like I was the worst mother in the world. And at that moment, I felt like it.

"Son, didn't your mother tell you you're not supposed to call 9-1-1 unless there's a real emergency," the officer said, side-eyeing me.

Of course, I did. I also told him to clean his room, but he didn't listen then, either. Can you do something about that? I wanted to shout. But I stood there looking pitiful.

"Well, if not being able to watch *Power Rangers* isn't an emergency, I don't know what is," Myles said matter-of-factly.

I immediately began apologizing. Police officer number one

flashed a comforting smile. "It's okay. We've seen this situation before."

But number two continued shaking his head in disgust.

I walked the officers out, came back in and sat my children down and gave them the dos and don'ts of the telephone.

We'd just wrapped up our conversation when the sitter bounced down the stairs.

"Hey, what's going on?" she asked, clueless.

I simply stared at her, trying to form the words "You're fired." But since she was the reason I was able to get half the stuff I needed done, I simply said, "I think I need a drink."

Countdown 'Til College...

Dear Diary,

Is there something wrong with me? I see all these people on television talking about how the time with their kids flew by. I see mothers in tears as they drop their babies off at college. I dream of college, too. But in my dreams, I slow down just long enough to push my kid out on the sidewalk and keep it moving...

June 15, 2025.

That month is burned in my brain. It is a significant day in my life. That's the day my last child will graduate from high school. (He is in kindergarten, but proper planning makes for perfect execution!)

So, I'm counting down the days. Sure the school district might change the schedule around; we might even move. But somewhere in that vicinity in 2025, I will be free. One of my girlfriends likes to remind me that it will just be the beginning of a new host of other problems, but at least I'll be free.

I don't mean to look at my kids as some sort of ball and chain, but the things I used to do, I can't do anymore. My husband always jokes, "I just want to walk around the house butt-naked." Now, he never wanted to walk around the house butt-naked before we had kids. But there's something about knowing you can't do a thing that makes you want to do it.

I've never been a spur-of-the-moment, last-minute, let's-take-a-trip-to-Vegas kind of girl. But now, I dream about it on a regular basis. I want to be able to go somewhere without arranging child-care, or figuring out what the children are going to eat for dinner or wear to school. Don't get me wrong, my husband is a big help, but there's something about that maternal bond my kids can't shake.

Like when I was in Atlanta on a book tour. Mya called me at seven in the morning, in a panic.

"Oh, my God, Mom. I missed the school bus."

Coming out of a deep sleep, I mumbled, "Mya. I'm in Atlanta. Can you walk down the hall and tell your dad?"

"But, Mom! What am I gonna do?"

I repeated, "You're gonna go tell your dad." Then I hung up the phone.

Why is it no one ever wants to bother dad? Take the time when my kids tiptoed into my room early one Saturday morning and shook me until I woke up.

"Mom, can you come fix us some cereal?" Morgan asked.

I groggily turned over. I'd worked late the night before and was exhausted. "Ask your dad."

"But he's 'sleep," they whined.

It's like no one wants to bother dad, but mom is fair game.

I always wonder at what age kids no longer want to be bothered and go lock themselves in their room. (I use that term figuratively because there will be no locking of doors in my house.) Now, don't get me wrong. I appreciate being met at the door like I just returned from war. But sometimes—every now and then—I'd like to come in and not have all the kids and the dog immediately up under me!

My friend Gee-Gee says her son retreated to his room at four-teen and she wishes she could turn back the hands of time.

"I know you say that you can't wait for that time now, but I assure you when the time comes that they don't want to be bothered with you, you will cry because they're too busy with their own lives, plans, friends, etc. to bother you anymore," she said. "We miss our children when they become too busy. Now that my son is in college in another town (two hours away), I am lucky if I get a text once every two weeks! My heart breaks every time I think of him because I miss him SO MUCH!"

Yeah, okay.

Seriously, I have no doubt I'll miss my kids. But that's when I'll pick up the phone, and call, or go for a visit. But the beauty will be that I get to go back home. Alone.

My friend Kelley suggests setting some ground rules to get that "me" time I so desperately crave.

"You should set some ground rules for nondisturbance when you go to your room to rest, bathe or whatever. Just ask them to give you certain times for privacy and peace so that you are not overwhelmed."

Kelley's been reading too many parenting books.

I tease her, but I know she's right about one thing, treasure the time—good or bad.

"We have to learn to treasure all our times with them, even the turbulent ones because once they are gone, you can't get them back," Kelley said. "This may seem foreign right now because I remember how I felt when it was told to me, but now I'm on the other side."

I understand what Kelley is saying. Still, I can't wait to get to the other side.

I'm quite sure that breaking free of kids is not what Dr. Martin Luther King, Jr. had in mind when he crafted his letter from the Washington Monument. But I can't wait for the day when I drop my last kid at school, when I can say, "Free at last; free at last. Thank God, Almighty, I am free at last."

Motherhood in the New Millennium

Nov. 1, 1986

Dear Diary,

I make you this promise. When I have kids, I'm not going to tell them to do stuff just "because I said so." I'm going to be their friend. I'm going to respect their privacy. If they have a sign on their door that says "Knock before entering," I'm going to knock before entering. All things that my mother won't do! As I write, I'm staring out into the hallway. You wanna know why? Because she took the hinges off and removed the door! Who does that??? My mom, that's who! Just because I slammed the door when she told me I couldn't go to the party that everyone is going to. I was so mad that I slammed and locked the door. Once she found out it was locked, you would've sworn I'd committed some kind of major crime. I couldn't even get out the bed to unlock the door before she was coming with a screwdriver. When I have kids, that's not going to be me. I'm going to respect their privacy and understand that sometimes you don't have to be a mother; sometimes you can be a friend.

This has to be one of the absolute funniest passages of my diary. I don't know what's more funny, the fact that I actually believed this when I wrote it or the fact that this was one of the passages my mother overlooked.

Yes, my mother read my diary. Not only did she read my diary, she made notes in my diary. Here's one entry I had about some little boy I was crushing on.

Dear Diary,

I'm going to marry Cedric and live in a gigantic three-bedroom house and he's gonna buy us a nice Toyota Corolla. By then, he'll be manager at AutoZone. We're going to be so happy.

My mother wrote with a red pen in big, bold letters:

Really? The best you can aim for is a Toyota Corolla and AutoZone??? PS—that boy is no good!

Most moms, if they did read the diary, would've read it and put it away. But not mine. She made notes and highlights all throughout the diary, so I swore that wouldn't be me. I was going to be a modern-day mom.

That lasted until my first child could talk back to me; when that happened, I turned into my mother. I still have splinters from when I kicked the door in when my child had a Disney Channel "I hate my life moment" and slammed my door.

I came to see that mothering in the New Millennium not only requires all that my mother did, but it encompassed a whole new arena of requirements, compliments of the digital age.

My oldest daughter doesn't have a diary. She shares her secret thoughts on Facebook, Twitter, Instagram, Pinterest and everywhere else. (Dang, wonder where she gets that from?) Well, she *would share* if she was allowed on those outlets.

I'll admit, I'm addicted to Facebook and Twitter, but I'm also social media savvy, so I know the dangers that lurk on the Internet. I know how to navigate the turbulent waters. Which is why, being the intelligent mother that I am, when my daughter came to me and asked for a Facebook account, I said no. I did, however, allow her to get an Instagram account. I sat my daughter down and talked to her about the ills of social media. We discussed the dos and don'ts and I explained that there would be consequences should she violate any of our terms.

My daughter was pretty level-headed and very mature. Or so I thought. Imagine my surprise when I checked her Instagram account (shout-out to the nosey moms). (Disclaimer: if you have a problem with violating your child's privacy, you might want to stop reading right now.) There will be no building of bombs in my house. I belong to the Nosey Moms Club and I'm proud of it. In fact, I recently saw a report that said that more than 70 percent of parents admit to spying on their kids' Facebook pages. (Question 1, when the heck did trying to see what your kids are doing becoming "spying"? Question 2, what in the hell is wrong with the other 30 percent???)

So, on this particular day, I was checking her Instagram account and was stunned—more like mortified—when I spotted my precious, smart, mature daughter, holding a big bottle of liquor accompanied by the note, "I wish I could drink this. Lol."

Needless to say, I wasn't LOL, ROFLMAO, KSML or any of that other teen jargon. I was about to go O-F-F.

Instead of going to wake her as my first instinct instructed me, I took a sip of that bottle of liquor (don't even start with why I have liquor in the house with kids. I have liquor in the house BECAUSE I have kids. But it's kept in a cabinet that the kids know they're not supposed to touch.)

After pondering ways I would punish her, I decided to hit her where it hurt most. I would utilize something my grandmother always used to say, "Where you show out is where you get to'e out" (that's "tore" for all you nonslang-understanding folks). It basically means, if you act up in public, you get disciplined in public.

So when my daughter woke up, I was waiting for her—complete with a sign that read: *"Since I want to post pictures of me holding liquor, I am obviously not ready for social media and will be taking a hiatus. Bye-bye."*

My daughter was mortified as she stared at the piece of paper. "Wh-what do you want me to do with that?" she asked.

I handed it to her. "Since you want to be posting pictures on Instagram, let's post some pictures. Smile," I said, holding the camera up to snap her photo.

"Noooo, please, mom, nooo," she cried.

"No, come on, Top Model. Hold the sign up, I can't read it."

Let the waterworks begin. Mya began sobbing.

"No, don't cry now," I said. "You weren't crying last night when you posted that photo."

"I-I'm sorry. I won't do it again."

Snap. "I'm sure you won't. But we're gonna post this for all your little friends to see, right before we delete your account." *Snap.*

My daughter bawled like I'd never seen before. I was not moved. She begged me to punish her, take her phone, banish her to her room, "beat her," anything "but that."

Her pleas let me know I was doing the right thing. Her defense was she "didn't see the big deal because she wasn't actually drinking." She was "just trying to be cool."

That alone was my problem: *you didn't see anything wrong with it.* But today, it's an unopened bottle of liquor. At sixteen, it's a two-piece bikini with a banana in your mouth that you think is okay "because you were just kidding around." No. I needed to show her the seriousness of her actions and remind her of our previous conversation that violation of social media rules would come with consequences. Sure, I could've "kept it private" as many people said. But NOTHING would've gotten the severity of my message across except hitting her where it hurt most—in the very arena she chose to "show out."

I posted the photo to her Instagram account (I did cut off her face so you couldn't identify her.) Then, I posted it on my private Facebook page (with about 2,000 friends) as a warning to other parents to monitor their kids' social media accounts.

Well, I quickly learned there was no such thing as "private" on the World Wide Web. About thirty minutes after posting, I called my friend Victoria and said, "Girl, this photo I posted on my page has been shared two-hundred times."

She logged on and replied, "You mean *two thousand*?"

That's right, in less than an hour, the photo had been shared more than 2,000 times. I was dumbfounded. By the end of the day, it had been shared over 11,000 times from my page alone.

Never in a million years did I expect the photo to go viral, but I really am okay that it did as it served as an eye-opener for thousands of parents. And believe me, they sounded off. It became a hot-button topic on television, the radio, blogs, and social media. Everyone was weighing in. For the most part, people were supportive of my decision (I'd say about ninety percent.) But that other ten percent? Oh, boy! I got hate mail. I was called every horrid name in the book. I was attacked personally (several people started spewing racist comments about my name), talk show hosts gave their two cents, and parenting experts said I had gone too far.

One teen psychologist even emailed me and told me the next time my daughter makes me mad, "I should not fuss, yell, or embarrass her and should instead lay five grapes on the table, slowly eat them one at a time, and by the time I finish, I can have a rational, productive conversation." She said I should ALWAYS do this. Umm yeah, I'm gonna pass on that advice, but hey, maybe one of you guys can use it.

Everyone from Ricki Lake to Dr. Drew weighed in. One lady

on Dr. Drew called in and said I was a horrible mother and I should be "ashamed for embarrassing my daughter."

I told her—on national TV—"I've never seen a tombstone that said, 'Here lies Susie. She died from embarrassment.'"

We fielded calls from *The Steve Harvey Show*, *Dr. Phil*, CNN, ABC, Huffington Post, media around the world. Some people even accused me of posting the sign in an attempt to get publicity for myself and my books. Now, *that* did anger me. First of all, I'd never use my children like that. Secondly, I have a Facebook Fan Page with 13,000 fans. If I had been seeking attention, I would've posted the photo there and at the bottom of the sign my daughter held would've been my website and contact information!

Other than that, the attacks didn't bother me. This was my child we were talking about. None of these people knew me or my daughter. They couldn't analyze what she was capable of. They couldn't assess if any "damage was done to her emotionally." They didn't know that long after they were still doing call-ins, my daughter had moved on, telling me that she was "glad it was this picture that went viral and not the one of her holding the bottle of liquor."

"I could've really messed myself up, Mom," she told me. In fact, Mya was so moved behind it all, that she started a social media awareness group for her peers to help educate teens and tweens on the dangers of social media.

Leave it to my child to take lemons and make lemonade.

But, alas, don't give her any awards just yet.

Later, while updating my iPhone, they asked if I'd like to import my contacts from social media. I pressed *yes* and went on about my business.

A few days later, I told Siri (the voice on the iPhone) to call my daughter.

"Send a message to Mya Billingsley."

To which Siri replied, "Would you like to send the message to Mya's phone, her email, or her Twitter?"

Twitter?????

"Excuse me! Siri, you must be malfunctioning because surely my daughter does not have a Twitter account. SURELY, after getting in trouble behind Instagram, she wouldn't dare create a Twitter account."

"I'm sorry, I do not understand," Siri replied.

"Neither do I," I mumbled as I dropped the phone and logged on to Twitter.

Five minutes later, I was staring at my daughter's Twitter account. Now, I will say that she hadn't Tweeted anyone or received any Tweets since the whole Instagram debacle. But somewhere along the way, when I said "no social media," should've come the words, "Okay, but I just want you to know that I already have a secret Twitter account."

I know; I know. That would be too much like right. Needless to say, my conversation with her regarding that Twitter account is not fit to print.

To her, the fact that she hadn't Tweeted since the Instagram nightmare proved she had learned her lesson.

Another loophole.

What I learned was that in the New Millennium, we have to stay one step ahead of our children—at all times.

I travel all over the country speaking to young people. They have secret social media accounts. To some of those parents who say, "Not my child." Yes, your child. By no means am I saying your child would lie to you, but I'm saying based on the hundreds of young people I've talked to, anything is possible. And even the smartest, brightest children get lured into the world of social media and many of their parents remain clueless.

In fact, there was one young boy on Facebook who shared the Instagram post about my daughter and said, *"Look at what this bitch did. If that was my mom, I would drop-kick that ho."*

Me, being the social super sleuth that I am, proceeded to track down this boy's parents, whom I emailed. His mother called me and told me I must be mistaken because she and her husband were prominent ministers and their son only had one Facebook account, which they monitored. Long story short, that post had been posted on her son's *second page.* The one where he let his hair down, shed his choirboy image, and let the world know how much of a "tough thug" he really was. His parents were horrified at their son's alter ego.

One of the things I'm most proud of is the number of parents who were motivated by my actions to take a second look, and in some cases a first look. They found children they didn't recognize, inappropriate pictures, status updates, things that could drastically alter someone's life.

But perhaps the most riveting email came from a woman who wrote: *"My daughter lost her college scholarship because of some inappropriate pictures she posted on Facebook. She had a full ride and would have been the first person in our family to go to college. I wish I had been a nosey mom."*

I got other responses such as, *"Oh, I monitor my kid's computer usage,"* or *"My kids are only on the computer in the family room, so I can see what they're doing."*

Well, they get to school and they get on a friend's phone or iPad or laptop, so it's hard to monitor 24-7. That's why it's crucial to have a conversation. It doesn't mean you have a bad child because they get caught up in social media. Trust me, I know. But this is the age in which they live.

If you have children between the ages of eight and eighteen, you need to be talking to them about social media. And not just talking. You need to be savvy yourself. So many parents say, "Oh, I can't work those computers and I don't know much about social media." If you have kids, you need to get to know it. And you have to stay on top of things. Just when you learn MySpace, along comes Facebook. Got Facebook down, here comes Twitter. Tackle Twitter, here comes Pinterest. It's ever-evolving and you have to stay in the game.

So talk, then talk some more. Then join the Nosey Moms Club. Membership never closes!

Sometimes I Get It Right

March 3, 1987
Dear Diary,
Can you believe my mom locked me out of the house? I mean, really put the chain on the door and everything. Just because I missed curfew. Again. I'm never going to do something so cruel to my kids.

It's amazing, now anyway, how cruel I thought my mother was. As a teen I thought she was extremely strict, mainly because my friends could stay out as long as they wanted, and I had to be in by midnight. I swore that I was going to have more flexibility with my children. I was going to trust them and give them freedom.

That was then. This is now.

Oh, I trust my children. It's the other nutcases out there that I don't trust. And even my trust for my children will only go so far. I know the lure of peers, society, etc., can make even the most intelligent of children waver. But when all is said and done, all I can do is raise my kids to make healthy and wise decisions—even when Mama is nowhere around.

SIBLING RIVALRY

It's hard for me to relate to the way my kids fight. Growing up, I probably can count on one hand the number of fights I had with my sister. (I'm sure the fact that she did whatever I asked her to do, whenever I asked her to do it, had something to do with that.)

But that's why it is so hard for me to relate to the ongoing fights of my children. And it drives me crazy to see Mya torturing her little sister.

Like recently.

My sweet baby girl came home, smiling, a glow all over her face.

"Well, what's that look for?" I asked.

She giggled. "If I tell you, you promise not to get mad?"

(Who has that ever worked for?) "I promise," I said.

More giggles. "Antone likes me."

Clutch heart now. She's ten. And she really was about to tell me about some boy?

"Sweetie, you're too young to be thinking about boys."

"But, Mom. He really likes me."

Deep sigh. "Okay, honey, how do you know that?"

"He said I have athlete's feet."

Crickets.

"Excuse me?" I finally managed to say.

"He said I have athlete's feet," she proudly repeated. "Meaning, I'm good at athletics."

More crickets, interrupted by the howling laughter of my oldest daughter.

I tried to shoot Mya a chastising look, but I was trying not to laugh myself.

"OMG!" Mya howled. "She thinks athlete's feet is a compliment! Bwahahahahaha."

Morgan, oblivious to what was funny, frowned. "What's wrong with you?"

Mya, doubled over as she tried to catch her breath. "The question is what is wrong with you? Bwahahahaha."

"Mya, leave your sister alone! And go to your room."

Laughter trailed behind her as Morgan turned back to me and said, "Mom, why is she laughing?"

Now, what am I supposed to do at that point? Burst her bubble? Tell her Antone was a jerk and stay far away from him? While I was leaning toward the latter, I said, "While you are good at athletics, that's not what he meant."

I was about to explain exactly what athlete's feet was when someone knocked on the door. I went to answer and by the time I came back, Morgan was sitting at the kitchen table near tears. Strewn in front of her were the nastiest-looking pictures of feet that I'd ever seen. And Mya stood off in the corner giggling. She'd actually printed pictures of athlete's feet to show her sister.

I took Morgan for a pedicure—something Mya loved doing. But I made sure Mya stayed at home. The look on Morgan's face as she later flashed her perfectly manicured toes at her sister, said, *Who's laughing now?*

I love that even when I don't get it right, my children possess the initiative to make things happen for themselves. It's a tool that will prove beneficial in the future.

Take the time Mya told me she wanted to be a model. Since the inception of Tyra Banks' *America's Next Top Model*, every teen wants to be a model, so I didn't pay much attention to her. But she kept talking about it, asking for an agent. I kept blowing her off. Then one day, I got a call from the CEO of a major children's clothing company. I was stunned.

"Who is this again?" I asked.

He repeated his name and company, then continued. "I was calling because I got Mya's email."

This made me stop in my tracks. (Now that I think of it, my kids make me stop in my tracks quite a bit.)

He chuckled. "I wanted to personally call because while I admire her resourcefulness, we use an agency in Miami for our models."

Long story short, my child had gotten tired of my empty promises, and taken it upon herself to try and book her own modeling jobs. And mind you, she went straight for the top, managing to peruse the Internet until she found the personal email address for the CEO of her favorite clothing company.

I finally composed myself, apologized, and told him I'd pass the message on.

"No problem," he said, laughing. "You've got a whipper-snapper on your hands."

You don't know the half of it, I wanted to tell him.

I love that my children sometimes impart wisdom to me, without even knowing it.

Mya and I were traveling once when we spotted Stevie Wonder in the airport.

"Honey, look, it's Stevie Wonder. Go see if you can take a picture with him," I said.

My daughter looked at me pitifully and replied, "Mom, you don't want people bothering you when you travel, and you're nowhere near as famous as him. So how do you think he feels?"

I could only smile and said, "Duly noted, daughter. Duly noted."

MOTHERHOOD IS NOT A COMPETITION

My friend Lois is horrified by some of my parenting techniques, but since Lois isn't a parent, I take her advice with a grain of salt. And even if she was, what works for her child may not work for mine. Most of what I do—from joking with my children to posting the Instagram photo—I do because I know my children. I probably wouldn't have posted the photo if it had been my middle child because she's like me, emotional, lets things get to her. But I know my oldest child; she is what I wanted to be at her age— strong and resilient.

At one point, I did let the naysayers get to me. During the Instagram fiasco, some people called me a parental cyber bully.

One lady even wrote that *"when my daughter killed herself, her blood would be on my hands."*

The extremists caused me to sit my daughter down for a follow-up conversation. "Mya, you do understand why I did what I did?" I asked.

"Yeah, Mom," she said, looking at me like, why are we revisiting this conversation.

"I just wanted to make sure that you weren't planning to run away, or that you were suicidal behind any of this."

My daughter looked at me in horror. "Suicide? Really, Mom? I'm a Christian and I'm gonna be a top model or a scientist. How can I do that if I'm dead? And I have it too good to run away. So I guess I just have to live with everyone knowing I have a crazy mama."

I could only smile and take comfort in knowing that sometimes I do get it right.

Even my touch of crazy proves its point. Like the time Mya had been acting up in school and had the nerve to back-talk her teacher. So, yes, I was the embarrassing mom who came up to her school, belt in hand. I would've never in a million years used that belt there, but my daughter was losing her mind and desperate times called for desperate measures.

I pulled my daughter out of class, waving the belt as her friends were like, "Ooooh."

She was absolutely horrified. I told her "Suburban mom must have you fooled. Let me hear one more time that you back-talked a teacher and this is going to play out a whole lot differently. You understand?"

She nodded, grateful that this was just a warning.

That was three years ago, and we've never had a back-talking problem since.

That proved to me that sometimes crazy pays off. Even when you're not around. In the seventh grade, Mya came home and said, "Mom, you prevented a fight today."

"I prevented it? What does that mean?" She definitely had my attention. Number one, we don't fight, and number two, her school had a zero tolerance for fighting, so this story had better be good.

"This girl was all up in my face," she began. "She was going off on me and I just stood there letting her look like a fool while I said to myself, 'Ooooh, if my mama wasn't crazy, I would clock you in your eye right now.' But since I know how you are, I just turned and walked away."

Glad to know my craziness keeps her out of trouble!

For all my joking, all my humor, my children know that, at the end of the day, I have their best interest at heart, and all that I do, I do for them. So while I sometimes get it right, I don't kick myself for the times I get it wrong. And I don't get comfortable the times that I do. I know that at the end of the day, I may not be the perfect mother. but I'm giving them the best that I've got. And I'm going to spend the rest of my life reminding them of that. If I didn't, what kind of mother would I really be?

Motherhood Diaries

Along my mothering journey, there are so many times when I felt like I was so alone…when I wondered if I was the only good/mediocre/horrible mother on earth. But I got comfort from my sister-moms—those women who helped me see I wasn't in this thing alone.

So I wanted you to have a chance to hear from them.

When I made the call for mothers to share their stories, I was astonished at the feedback. And quite frankly, overwhelmed with the volume of submissions. But our team pored through the stories to find some of the best (I hate that we couldn't use them all.) These stories tugged at my heart and inspired me on my ongoing motherhood journey.

I hope you'll read each and every story. I'm sure one will resonate, touch your spirit, or offer you insight, all while inspiring and entertaining. (And if they've provided their website or contact information, please check out their other work and let them know what you think of their stories.) Oh, and when you're finished, share your own humorous, insightful, inspiring, or entertaining story at www.themotherhooddiaries.com.

Enjoy. I know I did!

Diary of the Overachieving Mom
(Who Longs for a Drink)
BY SADEQA JOHNSON

It's 5:26 p.m. and I'm hiding from my children in my closet. I'm all the way in the back, behind the tan wool coat that my second mother bought me when I was working in corporate America. The coat that has been covered in plastic for the past nine years, since I traded in my pumps and suits for a wardrobe of cargo pants and clogs. My head bobs against the slinky, black, halter dress with the amber brooch that became too tight, two pregnancies ago. I'm squatted on top of the tap shoes that I insist on keeping, just in case. Just in case I wake up one day and have a personal life. If I wasn't so damned responsible, I'd have a bottle of hard liquor hidden here, in a crumpled paper bag to slurp down on days like these, when I feel like I'm suffocating in my own skin.

The kids have wrecked my last nerve. And when I say nerve, I mean that piece of me that allows me to think straight, be calm and happy, grin and bear it, but I'm past that point today. Way past it. It's scary how past it I am. I'm so past it that I've broken the golden rule of a school night, and have allowed my three to watch a show on Disney. If I didn't walk away, I was going to shake, spank, or slap someone silly, and I don't want to be that mama. So I'm in the closet, hiding, trying to breathe in white light and choke out black smoke, trying to channel the energy of my higher serene self, trying to figure out how I keep getting to this point.

I've been a mother for nine years and it's my own fault that I didn't pace myself from the start. Instead, I piled it all on as high as a double-decker sandwich complete with toppings so thick, that I can no longer wrap my lips around it. When my eldest child, Miles, was six weeks old, I took him on a twenty-minute ride from our home to Gymboree. The class description said the group was for ages six weeks and up, designed to stimulate through tummy-time and flashlight play. I, the overachieving new mommy, wanted to make sure my son was on the right path from the start. This trip was literally my first time venturing out of the house with him, and I was so nervous that I got turned around twice. When we walked in, the other mothers and children were in full swing. It was winter, so I had to undo all of our layers and when we joined the circle, Miles was fast asleep. Dressed in his cute sweater outfit that was more fit for Christmas pictures than Gymboree, his eyes remained closed.

The teacher tried to stimulate him with scarves, puppets and bright colored balls, but he wouldn't wake. He was the youngest in the class by at least three months, so when she suggested I bring him back when he was a little older, I flushed with embarrassment as all eyes were on me and my too-young child. I bundled us back up and made it to the car before my floodgate opened and the tears plummeted.

I was lonely. My friends were at work, my husband was at work, and I was exhausted beyond anything that I could express. I had mastitis in my left breast and it was constantly engorged from not draining properly, so I worried if Miles had enough to eat. As I massaged my breast and prayed for it to produce, my mother said ridiculous things like, "Maybe he can't take the titty. Maybe you're not producing enough milk. Give that baby a bottle before he starves."

It was the last thing I wanted to hear and I never took her advice. The easy way has never been my way on this journey of motherhood, and I often wonder if the problem is the kids or over-reaching me. I've back-flipped, somersaulted and cartwheeled into this mommy-hood world, obsessed with getting it right. With goals of elevating us and making the kids well versed and well rounded, with credentials that look good on paper. I hope these things will make their lives less challenging than what my husband and I have had to endure, starting from scratch with no connections, mentors or help. And with the Obamas in the White House, my mantra has become, why not? Why not me? Why not my children?

I watch them with hawk eyes, looking for what they excel at and then enroll them in what I think is the appropriate class. My youngest daughter, Lena, named after Lena Horne, thinks that she is the next Chyna Ann McClain from the Disney show *A.N.T. Farm*. When she likes a song, she has to hear it ten times an hour. When Lena dances, it radiates from her soul and everything is moving. I'm talking about head, hips, shoulders, and feet. So I enrolled her in dance class, but not the one with the cutesy recitals and adorable pictures in frilly costumes. I chose the school where the director graduated from Julliard and is turning out prima ballerinas by the handful, even if it means driving thirty minutes on a Saturday morning when I'd rather be asleep. Did I mention that she's only four, and my husband thinks the cheaper class at the YMCA down the street would be just fine?

I rationalize with, "This could be her calling, Honey. Let's make sure we give her the best start possible."

Obsessive, I know, but I can't stop. My Zora—yes, named after Zora Neale Hurston—could do a perfect flip at the age of two. So you guessed it; I spent many months in Mommy and Me gymnastics, and I ain't talking The Little Gym. But if I may take credit for something, Zora is now on the competitive USAG team and just placed fourth in her division.

Miles, and I'm sure by now you can guess who he was named after, is nine years old and a sports fanatic, so I drive myself crazy getting him from football to ice hockey to karate to basketball; you get the picture. Between all three of my children, every moment of my day is accounted for. I am an educated chauffeur with 800 fans on Twitter, but I spend most of my day obsessing over what can fit into my children's already too-busy schedules. My brain is sore from figuring out how to do it all and get them in bed on time. I wait for them to soak up all of this privilege that we are affording them and appreciate me. But they don't. They don't think that me bending over backward, racing around town, giving up my writing time to find vampire teeth and Halloween costumes for skate night is anything more than what I'm supposed to be doing. That's why I am in the back of my closet thirsting for a strong, stiff drink. I'm used up and have nothing left to give.

It's gotten to the point where I'm no longer interested in being on the playground, setting up play-dates, going to Pump it Up, Chuck E. freakin' Cheese's or pumpkin picking on a Sunday. I don't want to do the laundry, iron uniforms, fix another nutritious meal, and sometimes, sometimes, I don't feel like reading with the kids before bed. There I said it.

Whew!

Don't get me wrong. I love being my children's mother, and the unit of family makes my blood flow, but all of the expectations that come with this job are sometimes too much.

In some of my circles, motherhood feels like a sport. As I sit waiting for my kids to finish their activities, I have to endure the constant conversations of perfection.

"I bought her Halloween costume three weeks ago; why would you wait until the last minute?"

"My daughter is wildly popular; she needs a personal assistant to keep up with her schedule."

"My son has been top in math since kindergarten; they are thinking about sending him up a grade because he's just so smart."

"Angel is so naturally flexible that she is the youngest on the competitive cheerleading team."

These conversations go on and on and without my permission, I hear my voice chiming in with a one-up, until I'm standing on the rooftop looking down at myself wondering, *who the hell am I? What have I become?* Motherhood has given me a major identity crisis, and sometimes I feel stuck between who I used to be and who I am now. When I decided to stay home with my kids, I caught hell from my traditional, Philadelphia family.

My grandmother said, "You think you a white woman? Black folks work."

My father taunted, "What did I send you to college for, so that you can stay home and watch kids? What's wrong with daycare?"

I am overly sensitive about everything and my quest to show my family, to get it right, had me breaking out in hives after Zora's birth.

"Can I be allergic to my child?" I asked my OB.

"No, but you do need to take it easy and relax more," she replied.

I had only one real friend who stayed home, and I kept hanging with mothers who didn't look like me, had more money, bigger homes with gardeners and live-in nannies, and though on the outside I was hanging and fitting in, on the inside I was intimidated, lost, and lonesome.

My situation is unique because I didn't grow up the way I'm raising our children. My husband tells me that I parent them from a place of lack. Instead of seeing them for who they are, I see them with my little girl eyes that hungered and longed for my parents to see *me* and foster *my* talents. In their defense, my parents were young and had four children over the span of six years. I have rare memory glimpses of them being happy and in love, more vivid ones of them not. My mother and father spent most of their energy on paying the bills, keeping a warm roof over our heads, and sending us to Catholic school. There was no energy left for watching me with a keen eye to make sure my talents were tended.

My parents called it quits for the final time when I was in the sixth grade, and my father raised the four of us alone. Most times we were latchkey, and it was my responsibility to make sure everyone got home from school and did homework. When he could swing it, my father hired part-time help to look after us. Still, I was saddled with more responsibility than a child just turning double digits should be, and being a complete Daddy's girl, I did whatever I could to help him out. My mother wasn't around, so I was the mother for my three siblings, and I, too, wanted a mother. Now I am the real mother and I'm overdoing it, trying to get it all right and fix the mistakes that my parents made so that my kids won't grow up with issues. It's exhausting, and that's why I'm curled up in the back of my closet, thirsting for a strong drink.

"Mommy. Mommmmeeee. Mommmmmmmmmeeeeee."

My name is like a song on their lips and I scramble to the front of the closet and bump it open with my hip.

It's Lena, and she wraps her arms around my leg like I've been to Afghanistan fighting in the war and have just returned.

"What are you doing in the closet?" Zora is looking at me with her cute, scrunched-up nose.

"Fixing my shoes," I say.

"Let me help." Zora kneels beside me.

My spirit is all the way lifted in their delight of reconnecting with me.

"Can we have dessert now?" Lena fixes her brown eyes on me.

"Yes." I stand. Pity party over. Time to be Mommy again.

"Can we have ice cream?"

"Sure."

Lena pumps her hand in the air and says, "Yes!" Like she's just won the lottery. In a sense, she has, because she's got me, an overachieving, overloving mother who will go to any length to get it right.

Sadeqa Johnson is the mother of three and the author of the celebrated novel, Love in a Carry-on Bag. *Her second novel, which dives deeper into the perils of motherhood, will be released in July 2013. For more information please visit her at www.sadeqajohnson.com, on Twitter @ Sadeqasays and Facebook.com/sadeqajohnson.*

Diary of a Forgetful Mom
BY RAQUEL ROGERS

When I was a young girl, I was always losing things—my favorite doll, crayons, toys. When I became a young adult, it was the same thing—purses, jewelry, clothes would come up missing. I couldn't remember where I put them. It's a bad habit to have. I thought that I had pretty much gotten it under control once I entered adulthood.

I found out I didn't when I had kids.

Yes, I forget my kids. A lot. I'll pause while you groan, roll your eyes, and call me all kinds of horrible names. I deserve it. What kind of woman forgets her kids?

A woman like me. A woman that is already forgetful by nature, but throw in stress from working full time, raising two small kids (it feels like I'm raising them alone because my husband travels so much), and trying to maintain some semblance of sanity. I used to blow my forgetfulness off. But after I had kids, I started to wonder if I had pushed my brain out of my vagina with my kids.

I actually did well on my first child. I would forget my son's bottle occasionally and his diaper bag. And yeah, I forgot to drop him off at the daycare a few times. But I always discovered him before I made my way into the office building.

But with the birth of my baby girl—and the added stress of everything—my forgetfulness returned with a vengeance. Now, not only was I forgetting diaper bags, but I—I'm ashamed to even admit this—but I forget her. On more than one occasion.

The first time was when we were out shopping. I was pushing her stroller, where she was sound asleep and got sidetracked by some designer shoes. I moseyed over to try on the shoes, then moved to the next rack, and kept moving. It wasn't until about ten minutes later, as I was looking for something in the lingerie section, when an eerie feeling came over me.

"I'm forgetting something," I mumbled. And in that instant, I freaked. "Lily!" I raced back over to the shoe section and my baby was still parked in the same spot, still asleep. I glanced around and said a quick prayer of thanks that she was still safe, while at the same time wondering why no one had paid her any attention.

I never did share that story with my husband. He would've banned me from ever taking his child out again.

A few months later, I was in yet another store with my son when he sat in a chair, playing his video game while I shopped. It was a mega-sale and let's just say, I got caught up in all the great deals that I lost track of time—and my son. I paid for my purchases and headed out to the car. I actually was about ten minutes from home when I glanced over at my son's soccer ball in the front seat. Of course, I panicked and made a U-turn as fast as I could.

By the time I arrived back at the store, my son was back with security. I don't know which was sadder: the pathetic way the security guards were looking at me, or the fact that my son said, "See, I told you she would be back. My mom is always forgetting stuff."

"Stuff. Not her children," the store manager mumbled, not bothering to hide her disgust.

I wanted to tell her what she could do with her stank attitude, but I decided my best course was to say as little as possible.

I explained to the security officers what had happened: My daughter was with a relative and my son had decided to come with me at the last minute. I think that's why his presence wasn't registering. (That's the same excuse I gave my husband when my son blabbed to his daddy that "Mommy left me at the store.")

I gave yet another excuse to my husband, but weeks later, when I left BOTH kids at church (they had gone to the nursery while I enjoyed service), my husband put his foot down.

"Something is wrong, honey, and you need to go see a doctor."

I immediately became defensive. What if they said I had early onset dementia or something? Or what if there was some strange Alzheimer's disease for young people? No, the doctor wasn't the answer. "What's wrong is I'm an overworked, tired, stressed-out mother."

"Okay," my husband said calmly. "But when it gets to the point that you're leaving your kids, something has got to give."

I knew he was right. I had self-diagnosed myself for far too long. It was one thing to forget your keys, but when I started to put my children's lives in jeopardy, I needed to do something.

I set an appointment and went to see my doctor. Long story short, I had a thyroid problem that was getting worse as I got older. I'd never heard of that, but the doctor told me it was genetic. Then, it dawned on me how forgetful my late mother was.

The doctor prescribed some medication and I'm kicking myself that it took me this long to seek help. I can now shop with ease, knowing when it's time for me to go, I'll have my kids in tow. I haven't had a "forgetful" episode in months. Well, every time my husband finds a new outfit tucked in the back of my closet with the tags still on it, I conveniently "forget" how that got there. But other than that, I feel cured and I have my kids to thank.

Raquel Rogers is a freelance journalist in Houston, TX. The mother of two is currently working on her first novel.

Diary of a Mom/Dad
BY TANISHA TATE

When I found out I was pregnant, I had a mix of emotions. On one hand, I was excited about the little life that was growing inside of me, but then again, there was the problem of my "wonderful" boyfriend of three years suddenly morphing into "the boyfriend from hell." The carefree—and careless—loving man suddenly couldn't fathom the idea of another child (he had one from a previous relationship.) So much so, that he demanded that I get an abortion and if not, he would have nothing to do with the child. Actually, what he said was that as long as he "had to pay child support, he wouldn't be a part of my son's life." Now what kind of backward thinking is that? But, I digress.

Ten years later, he has held true to his word (for once in his life) and is not a part of his son's life. My son has seen his dad three times in ten years and he lives twenty minutes away.

That's my sad reality and enough to make any woman bitter. But I'm not bitter. I did what thousands of women like me do every day. I stepped up and took on the role of mother *and* father.

Don't get me wrong, I know no woman can completely take the role of a man in a young boy's life, but when you're left with no choice, you make it work the best you can.

Part of making it work for me is to move past the anger. Let go of the bitterness and focus on raising my son. That's hard to do—especially when you see your son's father take on the task of raising another woman's kids.

As a single mother, I struggle daily with raising a son to be a man in today's society. Although my son has several male role models in his life, I am both momma and daddy. I stay in constant prayer for strength and guidance as I'm sure most single moms do.

As my son begins to come of age, he has now started to ask those questions that I'm sure every little boy being raised by a single mom asks:

"Why doesn't my dad come see me?"

"Why did my dad leave us?"

"Was it my fault?"

"Why doesn't my dad love me?"

Now, there are a lot of ways that I could choose to answer these questions. If it were left up to my family and friends, the response should be "He's a piece of scum that is sorry and trifling" (to put it nicely).

However, I have chosen to handle things a little differently. When my son asks me questions about his dad, I am always honest with him, but I have chosen not to speak negatively about his father. Nor do I allow my friends and family to speak negatively of him in front of my son. That can sometimes prove to be quite difficult as they have absolutely no love for my son's father. (Neither do I, but I love my son and that trumps everything else.)

I tell my son that as adults, sometimes we all have decisions to make and that they are not always the best decisions. I assure him that his dad's decision to walk away had nothing to do with him.

The reason why I have taken this approach is simple. Too many times in the lives of children from single parents, their opinions of one parent are guided by what the other parent thinks. I am trying to raise my son to be someone that can form his own opinions. So however my child feels about his dad, I will know that they are truly his thoughts and not my feelings manifested in my son.

And believe me, there are lots of not-so-nice things I could find to say. I have to be honest, there are times when taking the high road isn't easy. Like on those rare days that my child happens to remember that the last time he spoke to his dad—two years ago—he promised to buy him a video game.

Still waiting.

Or when my child asks me, "Is it too late for me to have a daddy?"

On those days and in that moment, I have to take a deep breath and say a quick prayer before I answer.

As my son gets older, I have begun to play out several scenarios in my head. Because of the child I am raising, I can confidently say that he has a bright future ahead of him. Anyone that knows him, knows that he is going to be a lawyer, CEO, or even future President. I have played the scene in my head over and over of my son accepting some huge achievement or being sworn in, and his sperm donor showing up and trying to play daddy. *What do I do then?* Do I let my family kill him (not literally, but they'd like to give it a good try). Do I smile and let him take his place next to my son? I know what I will want to do. I would want to cuss him out and tell him to get lost, like he has been all of my son's life. But, I know that that is not the Christian response.

I have to let my child make that decision. I know that there is going to come a day when my son is going to tell me that he wants a relationship with his father. At that point, I can't tell you what my response is going to be. But I do know that it won't be easy. I am bracing myself for that day and planning exactly what I am going to say.

My greatest fear is that the day will come and my son will reach out to his dad, only to be let down once again. I only hope and pray that if that happens, I have taught my son to be resilient enough to bounce back from the disappointment.

And I hope if that day does come, my Christian response can rub off on my family. I hope so, but I doubt it.

Tanisha Tate is a teacher in Houston, TX. She is the mother of one son and a budding entrepreneur.

Diary of an Intuitive Mother
BY PAT TUCKER

Mothers know best, period! Sometimes, you must forget what the experts say. Doctors know quite a bit, but they don't know it all. Often, the naysayers are those closest to you in the form of family and friends. But, as a mother, there's something that you should never ignore. Perhaps you "had a feeling" that something wasn't quite right with your child, or you made a decision about your child that was based simply on a sensation that came from your gut. That's intuition—and a mother's brand of it can be very powerful.

My intuition told me early on that something wasn't quite right with my one-year-old son. He was a loving child, with big, bright, brown eyes that simply melted my heart. But those bright eyes could quickly turn dark with little or no warning.

Those mood swings concerned me, so I turned to my trusted circle. Our family doctor said, "Oh, he's fine; his personality is developing."

My in-laws said, "Oh, he's just being a boy. That's what boys do; you're just not used to having a boy."

My firstborn is a daughter who is four years older than her brother.

Reluctantly, I charged forward. If the people who knew us best determined there wasn't a problem, then maybe I was being a bit hypersensitive. Still, that nagging voice never quieted.

On the surface, my precious boy, the one charged with carrying on the Wilson name, seemed to be developing fine. Results from his well-child exams showed no indication of a problem looming, or reasons for concerns. He was off the charts when it came to growth, weight, and height expectations. But when I wanted to talk about his emotional development, people looked at me like I was crazy.

I consistently was told I was simply not accustomed to mothering a son. Could they be right? In my heart, I still felt something was wrong.

"He's just a boy; you want your son to be aggressive," said my husband, the Football Coach.

Deep down inside, I knew a toddler should not exhibit the kind of rage I had witnessed firsthand with my son. He would become so enraged by the smallest things that he would literally explode.

He would transform right before my eyes and begin a rampage of destruction. It was as if his little body couldn't contain the fury that burned in him, so he'd attempt to destroy anything in his path. During an episode, his little body was so incredibly strong, he would flip furniture, hurl his toys across the room, and rip things to shreds.

"Please, let's take him to see someone about this," I begged my husband.

"He's just bad! He's fine; his little butt needs to learn he can't act the fool and get away with it," my husband said.

Secretly, I began to research and investigate anger issues in toddlers. I found other mothers on the Internet who talked about anger issues involving their children. I learned about play therapy, and that even toddlers as young as mine could benefit from counseling. I also discovered that for some unknown reason, mental health professionals were recording a significant increase in the number of children struggling with issues surrounding anger and rage.

But my battle was only beginning. My mother's intuition told me my son was suffering, but with everyone around me, including his own father, and our family doctor, saying this was normal, I felt isolated.

When I again suggested to my husband that we take him to talk to someone, he looked at me like I had just insulted his mother. He was adamant; no son of his was going to talk to a counselor because *he* was fine.

Slowly but surely, the tide began to turn. Once again, I confided in the family doctor who apologized for not acknowledging the signs of a possible problem earlier. My mother told me to do what I felt was best no matter what.

But I didn't want to wage a war with my husband and his family. I needed to find a way to address this nagging intuition, but at the same time, keep the peace.

I made a series of phone calls to find out what I could do to get my son the help he needed. I contacted my insurance company, explained the issue, and requested a list of specialists in my area who could help. Instantly, I began interviewing counselors who specialized in young patients. Once I selected the person I thought was best suited for us, I began to sell the idea to my husband.

"What scares you the most?" I asked him about his reluctance to seek counseling for our son.

"Nothing scares me. I just think he's bad and I don't think there's anything wrong."

"But if there *is* something wrong, wouldn't you want us to do anything we can to help him?" I asked.

"Well, of course."

Sessions with the counselor were challenging. Emotions flared, and feelings came into play. Going in, I had heard how difficult this could be. I understood that finding out what was wrong with him, might result in discovering all that was wrong with me, with Dad, and all of us, but something in me finally began to feel at ease.

We are approaching one year of taking part in counseling. My son's rage episodes are not as frequent. As his parents, Dad and I are trying to use some of the tools we've learned. This is probably one of the hardest things we will ever have to do as parents. There are no guarantees, and for every step we make forward, sometimes we fall two or three behind. It's frustrating, and harder than we'd ever imagined.

But I now sleep better at night because when that nagging intuition pointed at a potential problem, I fought against the odds, and championed for my child. We still have a very long way to go before we can say he's 100 percent, or cured, if that's even possible.

While I'm not sure what the future holds as it relates to his future diagnosis, continued treatment, and the road ahead, I definitely feel like we are on the right path.

This experience has taught me that even when I'm standing alone, on the least popular side of a decision, or when everyone else around me sees something different, I must stand firm on my mother's intuition. There's something about being a mother, and I firmly believe that mother knows best.

Pat Tucker is the author of stories that are ripped from the headlines. Her work runs the gamut and includes everything from social issues to contemporary to erotica. The mother of two can be reached at www. authorpattucker.com.

Diary of a Special Needs Mother
BY EDNA PITTMAN

I am on a journey I never planned. Not even in my wildest dreams.

I'll never forget the day I got the call that would change my life forever. My precious three-year-old son, the joy of my life, had been forgotten in a hot van by his daycare center. That one fateful move turned my world upside down. That one tragic move left my son brain-damaged and made me the mother of a Special Needs child.

Initially, I felt shock, denial, grief, guilt, and anger. How could this happen to my child? Was I being punished for some sin I had committed when I was young? These were some of the questions that plagued my mind each day for months. I can't remember when I got over it, but when I did, I realized I had this wonderful little boy in front of me who needed me more now than ever before.

My son was born healthy and normal. He is my third child, my youngest, my only boy. One day, one mistake, changed his life forever. My once active, rough little boy was now totally dependent on me for everything. He could no longer walk, talk, feed himself, or even sit up. He was no longer potty trained, now suffered from seizures, and was legally blind. I was thrust into this world of the unknown. I had to buy new books, learn a new language, and meet more new people than I cared to.

In an instant, I became a nurse, physical therapist, occupational therapist, speech therapist, teacher, researcher and inventor. I had to learn patience that I never knew I had. On an average day, I do the same things ten to 100 times, if that's what it takes for my son to learn something new or accomplish a new goal. Although he loves the "Happy Birthday" song, he doesn't know when his birthday is or anticipate a wonderful party filled with friends. It's simply another day for him. While my daughters make a huge fuss over Christmas, he couldn't really care less. He doesn't know about Santa, and the gifts, food or traditions.

I've always considered myself a good mother; an outgoing, active person. I never thought that "doing it all" would mean doing all that I do in a day. I work overtime every day of the week. There's no such thing as sleeping in on the weekends. My son needs my constant care, so while everyone else sleeps in on Saturday morning, I'm up at six a.m. on the dot. He needs new bedding, new diapers, medication, feeding, bathing, clothing, therapy, and love.

I am a working mother of a special needs child. I never imagined how difficult that would be. I have guilt on both ends. I always have to decide job vs. child. My child always wins. I have to get him to therapy, doctor appointments, and school. As if I don't have enough to deal with, society sometimes makes it harder to have a special needs child. I've tried to gracefully manage the stares or insensitive remarks when we are in public. I find myself wishing people would look the other way. I know most people don't intend to hurt us, but they make us feel self-conscious and humiliated. Before I had a special needs child, I had more friends than I needed. I am grateful that for every girlfriend who has stopped including me and inviting my kids, I have added another who loves all of my children and includes us in everything.

Not many people are willing to care for a special needs child. It doesn't help when they find out that he was neglected by a daycare center and his mother is a "Hawk." By Hawk, I mean I drop in unannounced all the time. I call daily to make sure he got off the bus. I check and double-check when I pick him up, and if even a string of snot is on his face, I could lose it depending on the day I've had. I count his Pull-Ups to make sure he's being changed. I don't do this to be mean, but he can't tell me what is going on, so I have to keep a close watch over everything. I have two other children and no family in my town to watch them so the "Hawk" is what you get!

I have to make decisions that most parents never think about. I sometimes agonize over potential life-threatening or life-changing decisions. In five years, I've had to decide on several surgical procedures, whether to fire or hire certain doctors, specialists or therapists. I've made decisions on removing feeding tubes and traveling to a different country for treatment. I do it because I have to, and in the end, pray that it was the best decision for my son at that time.

While I know most mothers fear many things when they have children, mine seem to drive me to keep pushing, even when I feel like I have nothing left. I fear that one day I will die and who will be willing to take on the responsibility of my son? It's no walk in the park caring for him. He requires more equipment than a gym. I've had to learn more acronyms than a fifteen-year-old texting teen. Someone's lifestyle would completely change if they took him. There would no longer be spontaneity. Every aspect of his day has to be planned. They would never be able to vacation without finding special accommodations for him. I would never want to burden my other children with the responsibility, because they've already sacrificed a lot. Would he be loved or mistreated?

These things haunt me as his mother. I don't look for praise, honor or accolades for what I do. He's my child. I love him with everything inside of me. I do it not because I have to, but because I choose to. Yes, I choose to take care of him.

I'll never forget the day the doctors came to me and said, "You have other children. Caring for him will be draining, not only emotionally and physically, but financially. No one will think you are a bad person if you leave him here where there are nurses, doctors, and therapists who are trained to take care of children in this state."

That day I chose to take my child home, to love him, care for him, and help him reach his full potential. I chose to take this journey of uncertainty and to let the world see that he does matter.

While I think my role as a mother is sometimes a little over-whelming with a special needs child, it has also been rewarding. I feel that I know a far greater happiness, because I've felt a far greater pain. My child might not grow up to be a lawyer or cure cancer, but I know his triumphs give others hope. His smile has the ability to mend a broken heart, or brighten a day. He has taught me the meaning of unconditional love. Each day when he wakes up, I get to witness miracles that I would have been too busy to notice. When I look at him, I don't see a child with brain damage or developmental delays. I see a little boy, a great little boy.

Although I didn't choose this experience and would have given anything to avoid it, it has made me better. I've learned that a mother is sometimes faced with unfortunate circumstances. Although the pain of a dream lost never goes away, I choose to create a new dream. This dream, too, is filled with happiness, love, and a very special person...Demarion.

Edna Pittman is the mother of three. She resides in Oklahoma City, Oklahoma, with her husband and their three children. After her son's devastating accident, she worked with legislators in Oklahoma to get Demarion's Law passed. She is a Television Director and Founder/CEO of the non-profit organization BARI (Being A Real Influence). Find out more at www.Demarionslaw.com.

Diary of a Grieving Mother
BY LORNA "L.A." LEWIS

On March 21, 2011, my husband and I welcomed our third child. Kourtney Noel Lewis came into this world, four weeks before my due date. We were excited and disappointed that our beautiful little girl would not be immediately coming home with us. She stayed in the hospital for exactly one month. Thankfully, her stay was not due to any illness. It took Kourtney a little longer to learn to suck from a bottle, but once she learned, there was no stopping her. She had an appetite like no other.

Imagine how happy I was on April 21st, when the doctor called and told me she was ready to be discharged from the NICU. Finally, we were able to have our baby home with us. No more daily hospital visits two to three times a day. Once Kourtney came home, we settled into life as a family of five. Changes had to be made and schedules had to be revised, but it was a change that we were happy to make. We didn't know how much we wanted another baby until she came. She filled our home and our hearts with so much joy. I enjoyed the relationship that my children formed with one another. Like all siblings, they bickered and quarreled, but they loved each other unconditionally. My two older children spoiled Kourtney rotten. Whatever she wanted, she could have because she was the cute little baby. I so loved the way they felt the need to protect her and take care of her. Believe it or not, even though she was young, she also felt the need to protect them, too. Their bond was truly unbreakable.

On October 9, 2012, our whole world came crashing down. That is the day I walked into my children's room, as I did each morning, to wake the kids for school. I saw my baby lying in her bed, still not knowing that anything was wrong. I touched her and felt the coldness of her body. I moved her and knew instantly that she was no longer with us. The gift that we expected to have with us for many years, only stayed ours for eighteen, very short months.

The pain I experienced that day is one I could never really put into words. A part of me wanted to just disappear because the pain was so unbearable, but a bigger part of me knew that I couldn't. I still had a husband and two children who needed me now more than ever. It was during this time that I knew this was a burden too big for me to bear alone. I cried out to God and told him I couldn't do this on my own. I couldn't carry this load. It was too much for me.

At that point, I had to rely on my faith to see me through. I will never lie and tell anyone that this is easy, but I will say that I never once stopped trusting God. I know His love for me and I know His love for my baby. That love isn't one that will cause us to hurt without a purpose. God doesn't work like that. In my heart, I have to believe that this was done for our good. I would love for her to be here with us, but not if it means having to watch her suffer or go through any amount of hurt or pain. I keep telling myself there's a purpose for the pain. I haven't quite figured out the purpose, but I know it's there and I know with time, God will reveal it to me.

Right now, my mission is to continue doing God's work and be an example for my other children and my husband so that one day we will see our sweet baby once again. Oh, what a sweet reunion that will be!

One thing I constantly have to remind myself and my family is that no matter how bad things may seem, there's always someone who has it much worse. Believe it or not, death isn't the worst-case scenario. My heart aches for those mothers who have to watch their children in the hospital suffering for months. My heart also aches for those mothers whose child was taken from them by some unknown predator. For me, I couldn't imagine having to live through that torture. I know exactly where my baby is right now. She passed away unaccountable for anything, so there's no doubt that she's in Heaven.

Today my family and I are living what we call our "new normal." We know that life will never be normal because our normal included Kourtney. No parent should ever have to plan a funeral for his child, but unfortunately, many of us do. People are constantly writing me and calling me expressing their condolences and telling me how strong I am. They couldn't imagine going through this and still being able to somehow praise God. As a mother I will always long to have my baby with me, but as a Christian, I know that if she can't be with me, she's in the very best place that she can be.

Right now as I'm typing this, my baby is where we all hope and pray to be one day. I can no longer rock her to sleep. I can no longer kiss her sweet cheeks. I can no longer tell her how much I love her, or see that beautiful, dimpled smile on her face, but if I can't, then who better to do all those things with her than our Father in Heaven? That alone gives me the peace that I need to make it one more day.

Lorna "L.A." Lewis is an educator, author and mother of three. She lives in Baton Rouge, Louisiana. She can be reached at www.lalewisexpressions. com or via email at lladven@gmail.com.

Diary of a Stay-At-Home Mom
BY TIA McCOLLORS

Is this what my life has been reduced to? The question tumbled in my mind as I watched my then two-year-old daughter peer into the toilet and count the little packages she'd left behind. We'd almost fully transitioned from the overpriced Pull-Ups to big girl underwear, so completing this rite of passage was a huge turning point. I joyfully (and patiently) waited while she finished counting; afterward, we did the potty song and dance. Forget playing the Grammy Award-winning artists. In my household, this was our chart-topping hit.

I couldn't help but do so some counting myself. Even though I constantly tried not to think about it, I'd already calculated how much money I'd be making had I chosen to strap on my stilettos and continue climbing the corporate ladder instead of coming home six years prior to be a stay-at-home mom to my firstborn. I didn't want to miss his milestone moments. I wanted to be with him every waking moment, whether that meant after a peaceful eight-hour night of sleep, or after a night when I'd barely closed my eyes. Some of those nights, I stared at the ceiling, second-guessing this journey. Was I even qualified to be a parent? I knew my place in the world as a career professional, a friend, and a wife, but this assignment—with all the joy born with it—was heavier on my shoulders. I felt alone, separated by physical and emotional distance from my family and closest friends.

Being a parent makes you appreciate the village mentality. Unlike my upbringing, families no longer live in close proximity to one another. They're scattered around the country, making it harder to get a break when you've got two children with a vise grip around your knees. It's a struggle to escape to the salon, go to doctor appointments, or simply hand them over for a while when you need a moment to breathe. To exhale.

Even stay-at-home mothers need an occasional "time-out." It's the break I need to gather my emotions and huddle on the side-lines with my husband to make sure our children are headed toward their intended goals with their faith and beliefs as their constant companions. I wonder how the world will evolve now that most of the things presented to my children speak the opposite of what I believe. How do I shield them, yet give them room to grow? How do I teach them to take the time to establish their unique identities when everyone else around them is rushing them into cookie-cutter images?

My children are accustomed to instant gratification. The world opens up to them at the click of a mouse. They will never search for a book in the library using a card catalog, or have to wait until Saturday morning to watch cartoons. They've never seen a roll of 35 mm film or had to wait a week to see a photograph. We live in a hurried society, but the core values I hope to instill in my children can't be developed in an instant: Unyielding faith. Resilience. Respect for themselves and others. Book smarts and street smarts. Financial intelligence. Integrity. The list goes on, as do the lessons that my children have actually taught *me*!

TAKE TIME FOR YOURSELF. YOU NEED IT AND YOU DESERVE IT.

After ten minutes of begging, I acquiesced to my daughter's

demands to play hide-and-seek. I was deep into working on a new manuscript and didn't want to pull away from my laptop and disrupt my groove. But I knew her whining wouldn't stop until I began counting to ten. I peeked around the doorway after my daughter ran into the next room in pure delight. She didn't utter a sound, but her toes were peeking out from behind the couch. "Be very quiet," I sang out, as I looked around every nook of the room. "You don't want Mommy to find you." I went back to my desk. She was hiding, but I wasn't seeking. Finally, a little peace and quiet.

EVEN IF YOU CAN'T SEE THE WHOLE PICTURE, STEP OUT AND TRY SOMETHING NEW. IF YOU FAIL, ERASE YOUR MISTAKES AND START OVER.

One evening I heard my son bragging to his little sister that he could do his homework with his eyes closed. What a relief that his confidence had grown in math and I didn't need to hover over him. As their giggles escalated, I went to the kitchen table. My son's eyes *were* closed. *Literally.* I sent him to find the big pink eraser. Of course, I don't encourage doing homework with your eyes closed, but there's definitely nothing wrong with a little blind faith. Like the old saying goes, "It's better to have tried and failed than never to have tried at all."

YOU CAN DO ANYTHING.

The nightly bath ritual with my children gives us a chance to connect. It helps all of us to relax, and gives me individual time with them. By the time their fingers and toes wrinkle like raisins, we've discussed every topic imaginable. My son's conversations last so long that he usually forgets to wash himself! But on one particular night, he handed me a dripping washcloth and a soggy bar of soap. He stared at me with a pair of bright, four-year-old eyes and said, "Mommy, can you wash my sins away?" It nearly brought me to tears. That's a job that I'm actually *not* equipped for, but it was humbling to know that my son saw me bigger than I saw myself. You may not be able to wash away sins, but there are a lot of things that you *can* do if you put your mind to it.

YOU'LL NEVER KNOW IF YOU DON'T ASK.

My daughter is a master interrogator. There's no subject that she won't approach and she's relentless about hounding a person until she gets an answer she's satisfied with. One particular morning, she was concentrating on working on a picture, being careful to stay inside the lines. Her tongue was tucked in her cheek in deep concentration, but I could tell if her mind's wheels were spinning. She looked at me with a furrowed brow.

"Where did I live when you were a little girl? How did I get in your stomach? When did you know it was time for me to go in there? And why does everyone have a butt?"

I answered the questions as simply as I could: "In Heaven. God put you there. God told me. Because everyone has to use it. Food comes out so more food can go in."

She was satisfied. Asking—and getting answers to—questions, usually solves a lot of problems. The woman who has held a grudge because her sister treats her standoffish may merely need to ask what she's done to offend her sibling. The wife wondering why her husband is stressed should ask what she can do to alleviate his daily pressure. You'll never know if you don't ask.

PEOPLE MAY NOT BE WHO YOU THINK THEY ARE.

It was a sizzling summer afternoon, but despite the heat, I'd headed out to do some shopping at the outlet mall. I held my son's hand as we trekked across the parking lot, but he could barely walk because he was straining his neck to see behind him. I knew from experience that this wasn't a good thing. I already knew who he was staring at. Two Muslim women dressed in hijabs, their full traditional Muslim head coverings, had gotten out of the car beside us.

"Is that Jesus and Moses?" he asked, still struggling to get a better look.

"No," I said, attempting to drag him away. As luck would have it, after shopping we returned to our car at the same time as the women. I definitely see why my son would relate the two women to the illustrations in his children's Bible.

Before I could stop him, my son screamed, "Bye, Jesus and Moses! Y'all pray for me!"

I quickly caught the lesson. People may not be who you think they are. Look past their facades. You may end up finding a close friend, or exposing an enemy.

MAKE IT WORK. YOU ALREADY HAVE EVERYTHING YOU NEED.

All children go through a fickle stage. One week they want to eat bananas for every meal, and the next, they shriek when you mention anything about bananas. My two little ones are no exception, but I've learned to build my meals around their usual preferences. This Mommy has a kitchen motto: When all else fails, cook a casserole. As long as there's chicken in the freezer and rice in the pantry, I have the basics to get started. Usually, if I take the time to dig deeper in the fridge, or move items around in the cabinets, I find everything I need to cook a satisfying meal. The same is true in life. Financial needs can be settled by shifting things around in the budget. A dream can be realized by digging deeper for a boost of confidence and discipline. Do what you need to do to make it work! You already have everything within you. We all do.

I'll never be a perfect mother, but I'll strive to do what I tell my children: Be your best you.

Has my life been reduced because I sat in the bathroom with my daughter counting her packages? No. In fact, my children have enlarged my life more than I could ever imagine. They've expanded my imagination, grown my patience, and enlarged the dreams for our family. My son and daughter have shown me that life can be peaceful...especially when they're sound asleep.

Tia McCollors is the author of a number of faith-based novels geared toward women, as well as the non-fiction Prissy Purse Devotions *series. Above all, she loves to journal about the laughable and embarrassing moments of her two small children. She lives with her family in the Atlanta, GA area. Find out more about Tia at www.TiaMcCollors.com.*

Diary of an Abusive Mother
BY NORLITA BROWN

He was sixteen as we sat in the therapist's office baring our souls to her. He was thinking that he was right, while I undoubtedly thought that she would tell him just how wrong he was. When he spoke, I knew that he would bring up the abuse by my former lover, that live-in boyfriend that never should have been, and he did.

What I didn't know is that he would also tell her that he had forgiven me for that, but what he hadn't forgiven me for was the abuse that I had inflicted. I was astonished, to say the least, as my mind played over the events of our life. What could he possibly mean by that? I didn't abuse him, did I? What I did was discipline, right?

As my mind danced along the days of our lives, his words relived his abuse, opened my eyes, and shattered my world. I was a good mom. I had to be. Everyone around me told me so, but what about the things they didn't see? What about the time when he was only five years old? I don't know what he had done that had made me so angry. I remember wanting to "show him better than I could tell him" that he wasn't grown. He was a child and I was his parent. I looked into his beautiful eyes and before I knew it, I said it: "If you can take care of yourself, then do it."

As if that wasn't enough damage, I proceeded to walk his small-framed body out the door. I closed and locked it. Of course, I wasn't going to let him go anywhere as I immediately ran to the blinds and peeked out at him, wondering if he would be brave enough to walk off the porch. He wasn't. He cried. He pounded on the door and cried. Huge teardrops falling to the ground caused my heart to break. But my stubborn will had to make a point, had to show him that I was the parent, and he was the child. I let him stand outside that door for five minutes. In a child's mind, that is an eternity, an eternity of not knowing where he would go from here, or who he could depend on. My daughter stood silently behind me. She was braver than he was when I put her out at five years old. She actually left. She stormed right out the front door, when he was only a baby.

It was a cold Detroit day, yet that didn't matter to her. I looked out the window, the same as I had done with him, and watched her tiny body march down the street away from home. I quickly grabbed my son, threw a coat on him and myself as I rushed out the door, apparently not quickly enough. I looked everywhere. She was gone. I went to the home of a friend on the corner, knowing that's where she would head. I knocked on her door; no one answered. I panicked. I ran back to my home and called my mother. We lived two blocks from one another. I didn't have a car; I told her my dilemma and asked her to pick me up immediately. She did. We searched the neighborhood; my five-year-old daughter was gone.

When the call came in from the police station that they had my daughter, I was relieved. That moment didn't last long. The next emotion that would rise up and choke me was fear. Fear that my careless behavior could cost me both of my children. I rushed to the police station to claim my child. As I had suspected, they questioned me, my parenting, my judgment, my everything. I gave them the answers they sought. I gave them the truth. They released my daughter back into my care. They told me the neighbor across the street had seen my daughter go to the friend's house that I had gone to. Knowing that they weren't home, she went and got my daughter and then took her to the police station. I was livid! I wanted to call this person every name in the dictionary that didn't have a pleasant meaning. I wanted to knock on her door and tell her to mind her own business, next time! She knew it was my daughter. She could have brought her home, but no, she had to take the high road and take her to the station.

No longer was I mad at myself; no longer did I think about my bad parenting that led to this slippery slope because none of that mattered anymore. I had someone else to blame.

Now, I'm sitting on the couch listening to my son recount the events that scarred him emotionally. My eyes go from him to the therapist, trying to gauge her reaction, trying to save face, all the time knowing what the truth is and was, feeling my son's pain, yet still not accepting it. I was still not willing to believe that I am the cause of his grief. My poor judgment in parenting wreaked havoc on his life, causing him to make some very destructive decisions. He moves on to a different struggle in his life. My mind takes the journey with him, since I was present through it all.

For his sake, I won't go into detail with regard to what the issue was, but I will say that my son was dealing with an issue. I had taken him to the doctors who could find no reason for him to be having the issue. I then took him to the psychiatrist whose determination was the same as the doctor's. I tried talking to him. None of the methods worked. His sister, friends, and family began to taunt and tease him about the issue. I decided in all of my worldly wisdom that yes, let's all ridicule him. This will definitely help to get him past the issue. It didn't. What it did do was add to the wounds that had already been placed on his heart.

When he thought that his mother would have his back if no

one else would, I wasn't there for him. I joined the crowd and left him to fend for himself. I didn't want to let the tears fall, but they did. I heard his words ring in my mind, in my heart, and I was ashamed. Ashamed of what I have done to my son. I listened to his words:

Strength in words, Pain in meanings Part II
by De'Vray Rogers

Who put your hands around my throat;
who forced you to throw me out in the blistering cold
What made you right for blaming me for supposedly tying your hands
How did I give you no other option,
because before I can remember
You've been laying your hands on me
You have physically and emotionally abused me
How can you still look me in my eyes and tell me that you love me
I forgave you the first time only because you didn't know
But your actions were repeated, so I began to lose hope
Now that I don't trust you, you want to complain about it
But did I complain about the emotional scars that you alone put on
my soul
Tell me why I should trust you, just because you're my mother?
No, that won't stand as a reason, because you were also supposed to be
My hero, my protector, my caregiver, but you were on the other side
of the battlefield
Taking shots at me; you claim you're fighting for me, but I'm only
breathing because of whom?
I hope you can finally see why I have so many trust issues
And why I have a hard time trusting you.

Many will read his words and feel his pain. The mistake is the parents, who, like me, don't understand the depth of the abuse, or what is considered abuse.

My son wasn't beaten daily, weekly, or even monthly. In fact, I can count the number of times I put my hands on him on one hand. Does that matter? No, for him, the pain is the same.

We look at abused children as the ones who are getting hit daily, or who have a parent who is an alcoholic. We look at the extremes, but there are so many in-betweens that we miss. Our young men are being labeled incorrigible. Our young ladies are having children younger and younger. We keep asking ourselves what happened, refusing to believe that *we* are what happened. Somewhere along the line we forgot to parent. We forgot to put our children first. We forgot to love them unconditionally, to help groom them.

This is my story, my entry into the diary for parents like me who want to do better than they have been doing. Who want to mentor the young parents coming up behind us, to give them direction so that we can go back to that village that raised a child. It's time to give life back to our children!

Norlita Brown is the mother of three and grandmother of five. She resides in Georgia with her husband and son. She can be reached at www.brownessence.com.

Diary of a Single Parent
BY MARILYN DIAMOND

I had three bad boys. My eldest was eleven when I realized the "precious baby" was really a monster from another planet. When my boys were eleven, seven and six, I had to take a different approach to raising my sons. There was no "Look, the baby is going to school." It was, "Okay, this is the routine; you are getting on that bus and you better be on your best behavior. If I have to come up to school on account of you, it won't be pretty!"

My kids' friends teased them, saying things like "Your mama wears combat boots."

And their reply always was, "She shoots well, too!"

I was a full-time working parent and part-time USA Reservist, going back to finish my degree by the time the baby boy was in second grade. Little did I know that Baby Boy would do everything he had seen his two elder brothers trying to get away with. I had lots of support and help along the way. But it was me and my boys. When the eldest no longer wanted to play, the other two ganged up on him and played anyway. That led to the separating of the bedrooms. Each child had a different personality, each child ate certain foods, and each child played with certain people in the neighborhood.

They did have "Mortal Kombat" and music in common. I must say I relied on my eldest the most because he was the independent one. He would have preferred it if his brothers went back wherever they had come from because they stole everything, clothes included.

I didn't have much of a problem with my boys until they found out about girls. If one got in a fight, they all got in a fight! As they grew older and went to different schools, their personalities and the integrity, love, and respect they were shown at home became apparent.

As my eldest graduated high school, it was expected that all three were going to graduate high school and go on to college. Unbeknownst to me, the streets, drugs, and alcohol showed up for the baby boy.

My middle son loved the attention his good looks garnered and the women picked him up. Baby Boy felt abandoned and found a new family in the form of gangs. That life eventually led him to jail.

My heart breaks that my baby boy is away for breaking into another woman's home with an automatic weapon under the influence of the drug Ecstasy. I have dealt with the guilt of failing to protect my son from the streets. But I finally realized that it was not my fault. He is dealing with his consequences. It was a hard pill to swallow, that although I did the best that I could, I was only human. I have an amazing relationship with all three of my boys. We talk about everything, no holds barred.

My eldest is living his life as a Mason and a counselor for children suffering from bone marrow diseases. My middle child works for the Board of Education in New York. He also has allowed my mother and me to become proud grandparents of two boys and two girls.

Could I have done things differently? Sure, but who's perfect? Did my children want for anything? They had the best that I could do and their welfare was always covered. They are great men and I am proud of whom each of my children has become and are still striving to become.

Society says that if my children are alive, then I broke the statistical barriers of raising three African-American boys who have lived past the age of twenty-one. Knowing that, I think I did all right.

Marilyn G. Diamond is currently a book reviewer for OOSA, Sankofa Literacy Society and Delphine Publications. Finishing her first manuscript, she is vigilantly honing her craft in South Carolina. The mother of three grown men and grandmother of four, she loves to travel, read, and meet new people.

Diary of the Adoptive Mom
BY C. MIKKI

Becoming a mom was not something that I had put much thought into as a young woman, until the day the doctors told me that I would never bear children. A year later, I was married and adoption became the only option. I would spend the next five years accepting that my DNA would stop when I died.

The adoption process was fairly easy for us as an African-American couple. There were lots of people interested in us. Young women would call and beg me to adopt their child, but none of them felt right. In most cases, they would want everything from money to rent paid for a total of nine months. We wrestled with so many various scenarios that I became weary of the process. In thinking about a child, there were only two important things for us:

1. The child had to be healthy.

2. One of the birth parents had to be African-American.

There are many physical attributes that I had not put much thought into such as skin tone, hair, and eye color. I certainly didn't want to waste time searching for a birth mother who would look like me. I let God do the choosing. Secretly, I hoped for a young version of me to come along, but I didn't dwell on it.

Several months passed and we received a call from a half-Filipino/half-Caucasian birth mother carrying a half-African-American boy. We met her one cold weekend in February. I knew the moment I saw her that my son was in there. She had taken the time to write out five pages of questions for us, given us all of her sonograms and even the clothing her church had donated. She scheduled a tour with the hospital and a meeting with her doctor. A mature woman in an interesting situation, she wanted nothing from us, except a commitment to love and care for her boy. Within three days, we welcomed our son, Ace, into the world. Moments after he was born, the nurse pried him out of the arms of my husband and smashed the big red button on the wall. I had seen enough ER shows to know that this wasn't a good sign. He still had some fluid in his throat and he wasn't breathing. Suddenly a team of people rushed in. I fell to the ground, terrified. "God, tell me you haven't brought us this far and are leaving us now."

His birth mother lay in the bed calm, but praying.

My husband backed up against the wall and stood silently. Moments later, he pulled me off the floor and whispered, "He's okay."

Ace was taken to ICU and when all was settled, his birth mother said to me, "I think that was God's way of disconnecting him from me and reconnecting him to you, Mama."

It would be nearly twelve hours before we could hold him. We stood by the ICU window the entire night watching him. The next day, when I was able to put my perfect baby in my arms, it gave me a sense of purpose. I didn't care that he didn't come out of my body. Besides, it looked more painful than I would have wanted anyway. I figured I had the best end of the stick. Ace was perfect in every way, but I did have one question: "When will his eyes change to brown? They look a little gray."

In my mind, I was thinking, surely those Filipino dark brown eyes and olive skin will transfer, but God had a lesson for me.

Every day, I'd wait for Ace to wake up and would look at his eyes—still gray. Three months later, they changed to green and I was confused. So I prayed.

"God, I didn't ask for much, and I'm thankful, but did you really set me up with a green-eyed kid? Really?" I also noticed the fine, golden-blond hairs around his forehead, his arms, and legs. "Really God? Green eyes and blond hair? This is not what I ordered, but okay."

By the time Ace turned six months, we sent a photo to the agency that had placed him with us. The social worker immediately picked up the phone and called me to say, "Had we known he would have those beautiful green eyes and sandy brown hair, we would have added an extra fifteen-thousand-dollar fee." She laughed, but I didn't find the humor.

Socially, there were things that I, the mildly militant, Louisiana-born, Southern girl, didn't prepare for. Simple tasks became daunting for me. I did not like how people would dote over his piercing green eyes. People wanted to touch and kiss him all the time and I was not having it. People would call him "pretty" and I would sarcastically think to myself, *Great, I got the pretty boy.*

Ace had beautiful eyes, golden-streaked hair and long eyelashes like Mr. Snuffleupagus. No matter where we would go, someone wanted to give him something and I'd have to force them not to. I wondered if he was the only child born in the last 100 years with green eyes and olive skin.

Having a pretty boy came with its fair share of moments that I'm not the proudest of as a mom. I didn't want him to grow up thinking that life was this way. I knew better. But at the same time, people could be utterly rude. They would say things that started to wear on my nerves about how my son looked.

Ace and I were on a flight and a Caucasian woman tried desperately to probe my son's heritage.

"Oh my, your eyes are brown. What color are your husband's eyes?" she curiously inquired.

In my mind, I wondered what business was it of hers? I don't know you, lady, and have no need or reason to respond to your questioning. The Mama bear in me had been through this many times and little did she know that she was about to be shut down. I responded to her question calmly about my husband's eye color, "Brown."

Then, there it was, the look of utter confusion that I had seen so many times before. She could have stopped there, but they never do.

"Oh my, then wherever did he get those beautiful green eyes?"

I calmly kissed my son's cheek, turned, smiled at her, and replied with one word: "Slavery."

The old woman sat back in her chair and did not move or speak for the remainder of the two-hour flight.

When I would take Ace to the park or a store, inevitably, someone would stare. I would be asked, "Is that your son?" Or "Are you babysitting?" I began to give the most ridiculous answer that I could think of at the moment. By the time Ace was sixteen months, I had an arsenal of ridiculous answers as to why my son had green eyes. Once a woman at his daycare came up to me and said, "That *can't* be your son."

"Yes, this is my son."

"Did you cheat on your husband?" She laughed.

I was so angered by her question that I responded, "Yes, with yours."

She turned beet red and never spoke to me again, but I made it a point to wave at her husband.

In the grocery store, a woman came up to me and said, "My God, that baby looks nothing like you with those beautiful green eyes. Where did he get them from?"

I responded calmly, "The white man who raped me."

Flushed, she quickly turned away.

When asked, "Whose baby did you take?" followed by the usual fake laugh, I replied, "My husband cheated on me with a white woman who died in childbirth."

Of course, I know that none of those scenarios are the kind that should be taken lightly, but I was being so defensive about the questioning of my son. Perfect strangers felt they had the authority to question me and my child. I have never thought to randomly ask someone about their life in that way. It's no one's business and in my own way, I felt as if I was teaching them a lesson. In retrospect, I probably wasn't and should have said that he was adopted, but I didn't see Ace that way. I didn't wake up and say, "Good morning, adopted son." I don't introduce him to people by saying, "This is my adopted son." I say what's in my heart. "This is my son."

Eighteen months later, we were contacted by a young woman interested in placing her soon-to-be-born baby girl with us. Excited, we moved heaven and earth to fly across America to pick the baby up.

Ace had a nasty cold, so I flew to Virginia alone and picked the baby up. I named her Imani Christina. The next week, I traded places with my husband and he cared for her. We were waiting for the fourteen days to pass after which we could be bringing her home.

Virginia law says a birth mother has the right to change her mind in fourteen days and on the thirteenth day, that's exactly what happened. The young birth mother called to say that she and the birth father were going to get married and raise their baby. It was the most devastating moment of my life. My husband had to fly, across country, with an empty baby seat. We were so drained from the situation that we did the only thing we knew to do.

VACATION!

We dropped Ace with Grandma and planned a ten-day trip to Mexico.

Just as we were about to board the plane, a call came in from an agency in Louisiana. I almost didn't answer the phone. I assumed the case worker was calling with condolences about Imani, but she wasn't. She knew nothing about Imani. She had called to explain that they had not updated their parent books and our profile had been accidentally left inside. A birth mother they had been working with had not selected potential parents. Turns out, she had gone into labor early, but soon after, had contacted them and selected us. The birth father, a married man, had also agreed with the selection.

The case worker then hesitated because there was one problem with him. I held my breath and my husband's hand waiting to hear the problem. I know my limitations, and an unhealthy child is not something I wanted to take on. Carefully, I kept my ear to the phone.

"Well," she paused, "he has dark skin." My face scrunched up like a wrinkled piece of paper. I thought maybe I had heard her wrong and asked her to repeat herself.

"He has dark skin."

I pulled the phone away from my ear and looked at it in utter confusion. I still didn't fully understand what the issue was. She went on to explain that most of their African-American parents have no interest in dark-skinned males; they want light-skinned girls. She assumed she needed to tell us about it because Ace was biracial, and she thought that maybe that's why we had chosen him. I was mortified by the words coming out of her mouth, but I know that she meant no harm at all. I finally found the words to explain it to my husband, and his face was more crinkled than mine. While he and I share a caramel complexion, the color of our children's skin never entered our minds.

"Yes!" I replied. "We want him!"

She then went on to explain the "good news." Because of his skin-tone, the likelihood of him being adopted was slim and so he had been technically classified as "Special Needs." This classification would impact his fee—a fee that would be approximately $100. I thought back to the social worker that we worked with for Ace and her wishful thinking for $15,000 for his looks. I was deeply disturbed by this realization.

Is it not the content of a man's mind that makes him valuable? Is it the color of his eyes or his skin that determines value? As an African-American woman, I was mortified that we live in a society that has placed a label on my son before he has done anything in life. Society has told him that the color of his skin makes him less than and I refuse to accept that for him. I also refuse to raise Ace to believe that life will give him more because of his looks. It's something that I struggled with for years, but now, at eight and nine, the boys give me so many other things to think about, I can't worry about what people think and neither do they. The boys are grounded in who they are. We have told them they are adopted. They understand that, but they are truly brothers and they are truly my boys.

I thanked God for placing them both in my life because it was my path to raise them as equals and maybe somehow they will be able to make a difference in how people perceive and measure others. I'm so thankful that God chose me as the person to adopt. Sometimes in life we question why things happen to us. I know my answer to why I couldn't have children was so that I could have *my* children. Today, if asked to trade my boys for natural-born children, I'd say no because my boys are the best part of me. They are my pride and joy.

Author and filmmaker C. Mikki is best known for her sultry debut novel, Men & Sex Power, Pleasure, Pain. *She is also producing a ground-breaking documentary,* Black and Write, *about black literature and the publishing industry. C. Mikki resides in Austin, TX with her husband and sons.*

Diary of a Breast Cancer Survivor

BY CRYSTAL BROWN-TATUM

I thought telling my thirteen-year-old daughter, Jaclyn, that I had breast cancer would be the hardest thing I ever had to tell someone. For thirteen years, it was only Jaclyn and me against the world. Despite the tremendous obstacles placed in our paths, we always persevered and made the most out of what little we had. Together, we seemed unstoppable. But cancer can stop anything.

I walked into her room, sat down on the bed and took a deep breath. "I have something to tell you," I said.

She looked down at the floor and replied, "I know. You have breast cancer."

She must have overheard my husband and me talking, or perhaps she overheard a phone call. We hugged for what seemed like an eternity and then she simply asked if she could go outside and ride her bike.

That's it? I just told you that I have cancer and you want a bike ride? Well, ride on!

I really shouldn't have expected anything less from her. My daughter and I have been through the fire and weathered many storms. Knocking out cancer was something else that we would fight together.

At the ripe old age of thirty-five, I finally got married to the man of my dreams. Like my own father, my new husband was in the military and was one of the most honest and decent men I had ever met. We had actually met in college sixteen years prior and reconnected after The University of Houston ran a website news story on me. He reached out to me via email and after a whirlwind romance, we were married the next year. I relocated from Houston, Texas, to Shreveport, Louisiana, with a dog and teenage girl in tow.

During our courtship, I discovered a small lump in my armpit region while applying lotion after a shower. Although my grandmother had breast cancer a few years earlier, I never imagined that lump would be cancerous. So I simply ignored it and went about my life.

A month after our wedding, my husband encouraged me to go to the doctor about that suspicious lump that was now the size of a marble and had started to hurt. Ninety-six hours later, while on a business trip, I received the news over the phone that I had breast cancer. Looking back, I now realize that I was in complete shock the first few days. Rather than completely crumble, I decided to be strong for everyone else around me. Maybe I was too strong at times.

Looking back, this must have been a huge adjustment in Jaclyn's life. Not only was she gaining a stepfather, she was leaving a large metropolitan city for a small rural one. She never complained and did the best she could to manage all of these transitions. As a mother, I always wanted to put her in the best environment and sometimes that safe environment is simply in your arms.

My husband, Phil, did not take the news easily. Having very little knowledge and no experience with cancer, he thought that he was going to lose me in less than a year. I was sure that Jaclyn knew a little bit about breast cancer but assumed the words would have her thinking the same thing.

You see, my entire life has centered around my daughter. I became pregnant with her my sophomore year of college. Her father and I parted ways shortly after her birth and I embraced single motherhood head-on. I worked hard, sometimes juggling multiple jobs, to ensure that she would never go without. I made a lot of sacrifices but never complained because she did not ask to be brought into this world. After taking a year off, I returned to college and graduated with honors as I was determined not to become a statistic or have to rely on public assistance.

It is with that same determination that I knew I could overcome breast cancer. The oncologist told us in our first meeting that based on my cancer staging (IIIA), tumor size, and lymph node involvement, my five-year survival rate was in the 60th percentile. Without chemo, it was in the 30th percentile.

I decided to take my chances and initially declined chemotherapy. Let's be honest. I was thirty-five years old, a newlywed, a former pageant contestant, and quite frankly, I loved my long hair. The thought of losing all my hair was terrifying. In those moments of fear, I decided it was better for me to live out what time I had left content and with a head full of hair than to die from cancer anyway and have been sad and bald in the end.

I practiced my speech to myself and was prepared to tell my loved ones of my decision. Chemo was poison and I didn't want to put that in my system. I wanted Jaclyn to continue to see the happy, playful, and pretty mommy—not a sick one. Over the years, I had mastered the art of masking my hurt and pains and didn't want to start showcasing them now.

One afternoon, Jaclyn quietly came to me and said, "Mommy, if you die from breast cancer and you didn't do the chemo, I will never forgive you."

Wow! Such powerful words from a thirteen-year-old. Those words were the push I needed to embrace my fears and shed them. I drove to a salon the next day and had my head shaved. The stylist cried more than I did! I looked at myself in the mirror and you know what? I didn't look half bad! I had a pretty head!

When I got home, I walked into Jaclyn's room and removed my wig. I had started wearing one to see if I could get used to it. I will never forget the look on her face. It was a look of pride, sadness, and shock all rolled into one. She gave me a huge hug and said, "I am proud of you." She had never told me that, despite my numerous career and educational accomplishments.

Jaclyn was with me as much as she could be, considering she was a student. She tried her best to take care of me post-surgery (often fainting at the sight of scars and blood), sitting with me at chemo, and watching TV with me as I rested after radiation. To our surprise, her grades never dropped and her behavior never drastically changed. She demonstrated strength and courage way beyond her years.

I fought hard to survive. My daughter's harsh words were the driving force in my cancer treatment plan and my life in general. I never want to be a disappointment to the person I love more than anything else in this world. Every decision we make as mothers reflects on our children and ultimately affects them whether we realize it or not.

Lead by example, they say. I'm raising a fighter. Are you?

Crystal Brown-Tatum is the Founder and President of Crystal Clear Communications and the Founder of Sisters Network Shreveport. A graduate of The University of Houston in Radio & Television, she resides in Grand Prairie, Texas. She enjoys shopping for vintage items and spending time with her two Bichon Frisé dogs. She is a nationally recognized breast cancer survivor, author, speaker, and advocate.

Diary of a Wimpy Mom
BY KELEIGH CRIGLER HADLEY

Who would have thunk it? Certainly not I. Maybe you did, because you've held all my dreams, witnessed all my neuroses, and protected all my secrets since I was a girl. Maybe you knew what type of mom I would be.

Do you remember what a hot mess I was before I became a mom? I was great at ~~lying~~ using my vivid imagination to foresee what type of mom I would be. I would daydream for hours thinking about my little "Buddha baby." I wanted him to be chunky with rolls of fat so deep I could shoplift with them. I dreamt up innovative discipline techniques, untried and unproven, but in theory, they would surpass Dr. Spock's fame. Based on the sheer number of parenting books I read, I could qualify for a doctorate in child development. Despite my informal education, a nagging question remained. I had yet to determine what would be my mommy style. Although I desired to be unique, most moms fall into one mom type or mommy style.

I wondered if I would be the earthy mom who's a vegan, breastfeeds, co-sleeps, uses cloth diapers. She is so carbon foot-print free that she hovers, wears the baby as an accessory, and serves organic meals on Fair Trade plates that Ugandan women wove together. I had a special place in my heart for Sloppy Joes and Prada leather sling-backs, so earthy was out for me.

The sporty mom type is one who never actually looked pregnant and is skinnier after the baby is born than before, has play dates booked months in advance. Her day planner is organized down to the millisecond; she runs her kid around town in a $1,900 jogging stroller, and joins Baby Gym, Gymboree, Baby Yoga, and Baby MMA. I prefer the mental workout of a good book versus actual sweating, so I was not cut out to be the sporty mom.

The fashionista mom color-coordinates the family's outfits, hires a professional photographer/videographer to post pictures on Facebook, names her kids after designers on *Project Runway* and creates ensembles for each holiday (my first Valentine bib and matching onesie, my first Halloween bib and onesie, etc., etc.). I loved the idea of this mom, but it is a lot of work looking that clean, poised, and pressed. My way of ironing is hanging an outfit in the bathroom during my shower. So although I want to look cute, I don't want to do any extraordinary work to look perfect.

Then there is the crack-the-whip mom who is no nonsense, no frivolity, "no wire hangers!" She carries around a well-worn copy of *Tiger Mom* at all times, insists that her newborn will rise to meet her expectations, disciplines other children in the grocery store, and side-eyes mothers who coddle so hard it melts their PDA's. I practiced my "Don't you even think about it" look in the mirror but couldn't keep a straight face. Frowns give you wrinkles.

I didn't really fit any of those types, but I wasn't too worried. I knew that I would be above and beyond those clichés and stereotypes. I took a quiz on BabyCenter.com predicting my mommy style, and as we all know, everything on BabyCenter.com is the gospel truth, so I believed it. I'd be warm and firm. Loving and strong. I'd have the chef skills and craft finesse of Martha Stewart and the enthusiasm and endurance of Mary Lou Retton. Plus, I'd be artsy and smooth like Lou Rawls. I'd be a black Martha Lou Rawls.

I envisioned myself as a warrior mom, clad in fishnets, thigh-high, calf-skin boots, a Spanx-lined utility belt (packed with an iPad, Wet Wipes, Purell, and lip gloss), baby in a sling on my back, and a blinged-out "W" for warrior on my chest. My hubster, Mckinsey, and I discussed what type of parents we would be, and we knew that with a little determination and elbow grease, we would be the type other parents looked up to.

It was agreed upon that I would be a work-from-home mom, so I could readily juggle a husband, the kid, my job, housework, writing, church work and a social life. Easy as a double-back handspring.

D-day came and my robust baby boy was delivered on schedule, via natural childbirth. After a couple of hiccups with jaundice, we introduced our son to his new home and we accepted our transition from D.I.N.K.s (Double Income No Kids) to Parents.

Each day I awoke to a new purpose, a new passion and a baby on my boob. I had read all the books, so I was prepared for postpartum depression, milk leakage, hemorrhoids, and other TMI topics. Life was good; everything seemed rosier, sweeter, glossier—*insert record scratch here*.

Our son was almost two weeks old when Mckinsey said, "Imagine if Jireh had lived, we would have two boys now."

I nodded my head in agreement and murmured, "Uh-huh."

On the outside, I was nonchalant and calm. But inside, a horrifying thought resurfaced. One that I thought was dormant. *"Babies die."* It had been a thought so foreign to me. Old people die. Sick people die. Drug addicts die. Not babies.

Six years earlier, Mckinsey and I had endured the loss of our first child when I was twelve days away from my due date. The nursery was set up and decorated in strong, graphic boy tones. We had been given three baby showers and our small apartment was full of everything we needed, including an at-home heart monitor that I used religiously. We had decided on a name that I had chosen when I was fifteen. After reading *The Autobiography of Malcolm X*, I vowed that my son would be named after the charismatic and inspiring leader.

It was a Sunday, and when I woke up, I immediately knew something was wrong. I'm not the overly dramatic type, so when I told Mckinsey we needed to go to the hospital, he complied without question. We were immediately seen by a nurse who did a sonogram. Her face remained impassive and her tone remote. She would find us a doctor.

Two more nurses came by and did sonograms. Same reaction and response. I clutched at the hope that the nurses were idiots and the panicked feeling clawing at my insides was unjustified. I felt like I was drowning in a frozen lake and each person who walked through that door, with the passive expression of a serial killer, pushed me further below the icy water. The doctor finally came in and performed a sonogram, tried the heart monitor that produced a resounding silence, and then gave us the news.

For some inexplicable reason, our son had died. He recommended that I have a vaginal delivery instead of a C-section because the C-section scar would be a visual testimony to my loss. He didn't know that my stretch marks would serve that purpose as well. I would have to labor and push out a baby who would never take the breath of life. Never cry. Never open his eyes.

I delivered a physically perfect stillborn. We named him Jireh instead of Malcolm because I still had the hope of future children. We still have no clue as to why he died or what went wrong. We couldn't bear the thought of an autopsy, so we buried our son, in a ridiculously tiny, white casket and grieved together. I felt as if someone had poured molten lava on an open wound on my heart. I could finally answer the question, "What is more painful than childbirth?" Everyone felt so far away from me, including Mckinsey, although he physically remained right by my side.

The "what if" questions taunted me. What if I had been less/more active? What if I had drunk more water? What if I had taken better care of myself? Those questions buzzed around my head like a swarm of agitated bees, stinging and poisoning my thoughts.

I couldn't attend baby showers; seeing kids at the mall made me burst into tears; and I hated the thought of people pitying me. I would forever be the girl whose baby was stillborn. But it didn't really hit me until the first anniversary of his death that I had lost a son. I fell into a paralyzing depression and had to take a week off work to recover. Yet, as time promises, my wounds healed, the ice around my heart melted, and I grew strong.

Six years later, we were ecstatic to find out we were pregnant again. Sure, I had anxious thoughts while I was pregnant, especially as the due date approached, but my watchful doctor made me feel that everything would be okay. He went above and beyond, taking all precautions, and sure enough, Malcolm Mckinsey Hadley was induced two weeks before my due date—healthy, loud and strong.

But I was not the same woman from six years ago. I was a tad more jaded. A bit more reserved. When I was pregnant the first time, the possibility of a stillborn was not on my radar. Never thought a previously healthy baby would die in the womb. Now, I knew the SIDS statistics for every state west of the Mississippi. I clucked my tongue at any mother who didn't know the side effects of each vaccination. I was armed with knowledge and dangerous.

But the biggest change within me was not my Nazi-like stance on breastfeeding but my incessant feelings of doubt, fear, and worry. I naïvely thought I already knew something about worry. As if worrying about the arc of my career, the sag of my buttocks muscles, or even Mckinsey's safety while traveling, could compare to the nausea-inducing, heart-thumping fear I felt when I lay my son in his stuffed, animal-free, non-allergenic, CSPC-approved crib.

The waves of worry would make my knees buckle and weaken me initially. But then, it would morph into anger—a passionate, self-righteous anger prone to explode at the slightest provocation.

I developed road rage because of reckless drivers who didn't take heed of my "Baby on Board" sign. I blew up at nurses who didn't send my calls straight to the doctor and then called back cowering with apologies because I didn't want them to sabotage my child's care.

Although my son slept through the night by the time he was three months of age (don't hate), I was losing sleep because of the thoughts of SIDS, abduction, colic, autism and the notorious flat-head syndrome.

I even worried that worrying too much was bad for my health. I thought I was going crazy, like grab-a-cop's-gun crazy. I was on a cycle of worry, anger, despair, worry, anger, despair. The cycle was exhausting and I retreated more and more. Afraid to let anyone, including Mckinsey, take care of our son, afraid of public playgrounds, afraid of vaccinations, even afraid of household mold and mildew.

After one long night of staring at the audio/video baby monitor, it occurred to me, "I'm not the warrior mom I thought I would be. I don't deserve the blinged-out 'W.' Or better yet, that 'W' stands for something else. I am a Wimp." I had discovered my mom type now. I am the Wimpy Mom.

Frustrated by this revelation, I sought out the advice of other moms. Did they use a meat thermometer to check the bathwater? Did they pay for background checks on their doctors? Did they know the pharmacist schedule at their local CVS by heart? By the raised eyebrows and one, two, three, steps taken back from me, I took that as a no. Even my childless friends thought I was Charlie Sheen crazy.

One day, when my son was about eight months old, we went to my mom's house, and I overheard her talking to my brother on the phone.

"Don't forget to call me when you get back from your trip. You know I worry," she said.

I had one of those long, stretching, hallway moments. After thirty years, my mom still worried about her adult children.

I nearly slapped the phone out of her hand in my incessant need to get the answer to my question. "Mom, will you ever stop worrying about us?"

She looked at me as if I had just grown two heads. "Of course not. My cause of death will be Worry/Disappointment."

I gritted my teeth and ignored the last part of her statement. She had just given me a glimpse of my future. A future I wanted no part of.

My next move was to garner spiritual, timeless truth to free myself of a possible life sentence of whimpers and worry.

I Googled *"Worry scriptures"* (it's faster than thumbing through the Bible lexicon.) A bunch of worry-alleviating advice populated my screen. Then I typed in, *"Weak/strong scriptures."*

The first one to catch my eye was:

That is why I take such pleasure in weaknesses, insults, hardships, persecutions, and difficulties for the Messiah's sake, for when I am weak, then I am strong. 2 CORINTHIANS 12:10 ISV

Ah so, the wimpier and weaker that I am, the stronger I become? I needed more clarification.

I read the verse that preceded verse 10:

But he said to me, "My grace is all you need. My power is strongest when you are weak." 2 CORINTHIANS 12: 9A

Then I read one that tied it all together in my mind:

"…the Creator of the ends of the earth.
He will not grow tired or weary,
and his understanding no one can fathom.
He gives strength to the weary
and increases the power of the weak.
Even youths grow tired and weary,
and young men stumble and fall;
but those who hope in the Lord
will renew their strength.
They will soar on wings like eagles;
they will run and not grow weary,
they will walk and not be faint. PSALMS 40:28-31

I finally understood. It's not about my strength and what I can do to prevent life's ills. It's not about some caricature of a super-woman who can leap Lego buildings in a single bound. It's about acknowledging my weakness, my faults, and imperfections and allowing something greater than myself to be strong when I am weak. The scriptures made one of my favorite quotes all the more crystal clear: *"Worry does not empty tomorrow of its sorrow. It empties today of its strength."* —CORRIE TEN BOOM

Fast-forward four years and now we have added a bouncing (literally) baby girl, McKenna Drew, to our family. She falls off slides, chairs, stairs, and people, then brushes herself off and moves on. She once swallowed a dog kibble and dog poop within the same hour. I didn't make her down a bottle of Ipecac or disinfect her mouth with Listerine. I didn't call the National Guard. I simply checked poison control online and they advised, "Just monitor for signs of discomfort."

No need to call CPS on me just yet. I'm not negligent, only wiser. She is a happy ball of energy that needs to test the limits of playground equipment and gravity. Although her name means "the happy one," we have dubbed her "the fearless one." I still carry Purell, but I use it more for myself than the kiddos. Their immune systems are as solid as my faith. I now rock my blinged-out "W" T-shirt and I no longer care what my mom type is. We are all a part of the sisterhood of wimpy, warrior, weird, wacky, wonderful and altogether worthy moms who know where our true strength lies.

Keleigh Crigler Hadley is the author of the YA series Preacher's Kids. *She lives in Los Angeles with her hubby and two loveable kids. She's working to publish her next novel,* Revenge Inc., *in 2013.*

Diary of the Working Mom
(The Balancing Act)
BY MARCENA HOOKS

I really need about three clones: two for work and one at home. And while my clones would be doing their duty, I would be in the bathroom, reading.

Motherhood in this New Millennium equals being super-busy, and Super Woman since I am a working mom. I work full time for eight hours a day, five days a week. When I get off work, I come home to work some more.

What are weekends for me? They are just make-up time for what I didn't get to do during the week. Sometimes I feel like there are way more than two kids in our home, with all of the activities.

It's difficult to have a balancing act. Many times I feel I neglect my children because I go to work. If they have programs at school or daycare, I am there. If the programs are during the day, I have to take off work, which is a conflict sometimes. Luckily, I have a job that allows employees to make up their missed time via an alternative schedule. That really comes in handy during busy times when we have big deadlines at work. When my husband is out of town or has appointments, I have to fill in and transport them back and forth to school. If there is mandatory overtime on weekends, then that time is gone that could be spent with the children. Sometimes, someone or something gets left unattended or undone. We are only human with only so much time. We have to make up for it in other ways.

After school and work, the evenings go by so fast that I don't feel that the kids and I have enough quality time together. Here's how a typical evening may go for our family: playtime, homework, dinner (where my two kids almost always get in trouble), bath time, nighttime story (they fight over which book to read), and finally bedtime. Squeezing all of that in to a few hours makes us rush, but we find a way to get it done by working together.

Sometimes, I get so busy, I almost pee on myself because I forget to go. I'm doing laundry, helping one child with homework, while trying to watch the other child who is also calling my name, cooking, and checking the mail. All of this is going on while my husband is calling my name, too. They don't realize there is only one of me and I haven't caught my breath from the last fifty things I've been doing before they want more. By the time I do catch my breath, I'm collapsing into bed and might get five to six hours of sleep per night. This brings about another conflict for work: I'm sleepy on the job.

I've tried the work-at-home and housewife roles before and neither one worked out for me. I even took a class toward my Master's degree while I was off work for six months and home with my two kids. It was hard taking care of kids, home, and school, but I learned to study and read at night while the kids were asleep. It was hard for me to see how other moms went to school while working, but I realized the key is balance and having help.

I feel that I need to work, not only for financial reasons, but also for sanity. It nearly drove me crazy to stay home all day, work, and/or try to study and read, plus take care of the family. I feel that moms need adult time away from home and the kids for conversation and peace of mind. I get a lot of that peace and adult time at work.

When the kids get sick, I am a mom working extra overtime. The kids are clingier, more needy, and need more. This, of course, causes something else to again be neglected.

One thing about mothering in the New Millennium is that how we discipline our kids is so different; at least it has to be different in public places. It's a shame that our own children, or worse, a stranger, can call the police, DHS, or CPS on a parent for so-called child abuse. When my kids act up in public, I want to handle it right then and there. However, I have to stop and think quickly before acting and address it quietly but verbally.

A co-worker, who was out with her family at a restaurant, told me how someone called authorities on her. Her daughter was acting up and being cranky, so her husband took her to the restroom to have a talk. They came back to the table and she still hadn't settled down, so he barely tapped her. The next thing they knew, the police were at their table saying they'd gotten a call on them, *reporting* child abuse. The police didn't take any further action after looking at the child and clearly seeing she was unharmed.

I was shocked! I don't want this to ever happen to me, but I don't want to be afraid to discipline my children, either. I've learned to say something to my kids and save the discipline for the car or at home. My upbringing won't allow me to "just let it pass." My mom would get me where I acted up. She didn't save anything for later.

With the New Millennium, there's new technology. My kids play the Wii, want real cell phones, and have kid laptops. My oldest is only five, and has had a LeapPad for almost a year. I don't even know how to work it. I let them play games on my cell phone sometimes and my husband has put games on his iPad for them. This is very different from the days of playing outside and when girls played with dolls and boys played with trucks. We didn't have all this high-tech stuff. Time brings about a change and we must adapt to keep up with the times or get left behind.

This is my view of the balancing act: Realizing that our kids are different and learning to adapt.

There's nothing wrong with the old school way of doing things. We have to meet our kids' needs. At the end of the day, when my kids still want hugs and kisses, even after they get in trouble; or when they do well in school and make me proud; or when they do what I ask them to do the first time; when they draw pictures for me or share a fruit snack; and especially when they get concerned when I stub my toe or get hurt and then they pray for me; when they make me laugh or amaze me with their vocabulary, I know I am a blessed mom in this New Millennium.

I understand we only have twenty-four hours in a day. Everything on the to-do-list will not get done today. We have to make up for it in the following days. It's about taking care of priorities and doing what we can while we can. Working moms learn how to share themselves and divide their time. We have to try and focus on several things and keep our cool. Sometimes we have to choose between doing one thing over the other and decide what can wait and what can't.

Marcena Hooks is the mother of two small children. She lives in Oklahoma and is a freelance editor and proofreader. She can be contacted at marcenac @yahoo.com.

Diary of an Aspie Mom
BY MAKASHA DORSEY

He doesn't look like anything is wrong with him. I've heard those nine words spoken on countless occasions, in different contexts. There is always the well-meaning dental hygienist or educator who looks at me in awe as I explain to them that my son lives with Asperger's Syndrome.

With bright, understanding eyes, they search for something, anything, to let me know that he will be just fine in their care. Then, there are the judgmental words of relatives, acquaintances, and strangers who decide that I must be parenting wrong for such a normal-looking child to become so bothered by two kinds of food touching on his plate.

Regardless of the intent and tone of their comments, these are hurtful words to him and to me. He doesn't look like something is wrong with him because there is nothing wrong with him.

Justin—my little man with a big heart, enormous vocabulary, gigantic capacity for numbers, and supreme golfing skills—is an Aspie. Everything is right. Justin is exactly who he was created to be—my son.

In time, I know that he will be much more than that. But, to me, his mom, he will always be the bright-eyed, straight-haired baby boy the neonatal nurse handed to me moments after he was delivered a month early. The same little boy, who even at eight years old, has skin so soft it's downright enviable. The same little boy who, when he relaxes, reveals traces of his baby face, providing me with memories of staring into that beautiful face during late-night feedings.

From the moment I found out I was pregnant, my innate desire was to protect him from everything that could possibly harm him or prevent his growth. At mealtime, I chose the best ingredients from the five basic food groups, making most of our meals from scratch. When I cleaned, I used a steam cleaner and vinegar to disinfect my home. At play dates, I searched for other moms with the same values as me. We had plates of healthy snacks, child-proofed homes, age-appropriate toys, and large containers of hand sanitizer. If I was anything, I was diligent, focused on the whole child: physical, social, emotional, spiritual, environmental, and mental. My husband and I were determined to give him what he needed.

But I knew something about him was different. While Justin developed remarkably fast, there were some things rather quirky about him. He refused to walk barefoot on our perfectly mani-cured, insect-free lawn. He hated crowds and loud noises. He was absolutely preoccupied with trains and numbers. And, he had a weirdly unfounded British accent when both of his parents were from the deep South.

Of course, his aversions and personality nuances were blamed on my husband and me, the overbearing, overprotective, Internet-researching parents. We heard it all. "If you let him play with more children, he would be more normal." As if the children of our friends and family, at church, and school were not enough. "If you exposed him to more things, he would be more accepting of new things." Should I really let my two-year-old watch R-rated superhero movies? Should I allow him to listen to misogynistic and vulgar music? "If you fed him table food earlier, he would not have a problem with the texture of meat and casseroles." Was it really necessary to give him grits at three months of age?

As resolved in my parenting abilities as I was, I lost all confidence in every action I made. I began to second-guess meals, immunization schedules, toys, people—everything and everyone. I felt as though I was failing as a parent. In spite of my deliberate and decided efforts, deep down inside I knew that I was ruining my son.

On a somber weekday morning, in an aquatic-themed examination room, Justin's pediatrician listened intently to my concerns. Having observed Justin's behavior since birth, he carefully asked if I had ever heard of autism. Of course I had heard of autism; hadn't everyone? But my son could not be autistic.

At the doctor's own observation, Justin was shockingly advanced for a child his age. He was three and could read, for crying out loud. From my understanding, autistic children were limited in learning and language. However, Justin's behavior was indicative of a child with autism: tantrums, preoccupation with trains, fear of loud noises, and his unexplained British accent.

I was relieved and intimidated by the ensuing diagnosis of Sensory Processing Disorder (SPD), which is, in many cases, a symptom of autism. Justin's neurologist felt it was too early to fully diagnose my son, considering he was only three—especially since my little one had none of the physical indicators, such as tiptoe walking, clumsiness, lack of eye contact, and slow or no speech. But, SPD is a challenge within itself.

Children with SPD register, interpret, and process sensory information about the environment differently than their typical peers. Tactile, olfactory and auditory stimuli proved to be the areas that bothered Justin. Imagine a sense of touch so sensitive that you could feel every individual bump on the inside of your gym socks and a sense of smell so strong that even pleasant aromas caused you to gag. Or, not being able to attend sporting events because instead of the noisy crowd sounding like the 30,000 fans in attendance, it sounds more like thirty million. My real, most fulfilling, work as a parent began after understanding my son. A definition and a team made all the difference.

From the time Justin was three years old, he has had the benefit of a dynamic, although sometimes changing, team of professionals and his parents to help him be Justin.

Today, his official diagnosis is Asperger's Syndrome, with obsessive behavior disorder. He has gone from eating less than eight individual items to more than eighty items, which he has no problems combining. He has learned to manage in large crowds, eagerly attending collegiate and professional sporting events to watch his dad coach or our friends play. While he still has not grasped the kind of trust needed for team sports, he is an avid golfer, capable of driving a golf ball more than 75 yards. He matriculates with his peers in classes for typical kids, easily maintaining an A-average across the board. He prays fervently to *Daddy* God for continued growth, obedience, protection, and understanding. He is a loving and caring big brother, friend, son, and citizen.

As a result of him thriving, I have regained my confidence. While the words of well-meaning strangers or judgmental relatives still sting, I have learned the difference between my child's disobedient behavior and his disability-dictated behavior. I know what foods, smells, and situations cause him angst. And, I know that even as an Aspie, he has limitless potential. I am a mom who will continue to help him search after the things that makes him tick. I will remain his unyielding advocate, trusty confidante, and boisterously loud cheerleader.

There is nothing wrong with Justin; everything is right with him. He is an Aspie, and I am his mom.

Makasha Dorsey writes from home in Montgomery, Alabama—where she cares for her two sons in the most typical manner possible. You can learn more about her at MakashaDorsey.com

Diary of a Welfare Mom

BY LICHOL FORD

I am sure that the title alone makes some cringe. However, unlike the negative stereotypes that are portrayed in the media, I am proactively taking steps to become free of all public assistance. Imagine trying to raise four children in a society where emphasis is placed on material things. These very things often are the determining factor for so many aspects in a person's life—such as popularity and employment.

Raising children in the New Millennium is challenging enough, and to add poverty on top of those challenges makes it feel like an impossible task. On the other hand, my faith and determination give me the strength to keep persevering.

I often sit and recall how I tried unsuccessfully for almost ten years to conceive. After taking fertility pills, prenatal vitamins, trying various sexual positions, and other old wives' tales that people informed me would aid in the conception of a baby, I could not get pregnant.

Finally, I found myself asking God to open my womb and bless me with children. I said this prayer: "God, I come asking you to bless me with one of your greatest gifts. Lord, I desire to be a mother and have my own children. I've been a mother to other people's children, but I want my own children, even if it means raising them alone…"

After praying and praying, the love of my life became incarcerated, and I had yet to bring a child into this world. Once my mate went to prison, I stopped saying the prayer, and had basically given up the thought of having children. I figured it was my lot in life to be childless. None of my family or friends knew how much not having children hurt. Some even made comments such as, "You're not a woman until you have a baby."

Trust me, that is not something that a barren woman wants to hear. Finally, after starting a new relationship and with no plans of trying to have a baby, I conceived my first child without any fertility treatments or any of the other ridiculous things I had tried in the past. I did not try to get pregnant because I did not see this person as someone who I wanted to procreate with.

Fast-forward twelve years. I have four children by three men and the experience of raising them, although a struggle, is one I welcome and would not change. The only thing I would change is including these words in my prayer, "…raising them alone." I have learned to carefully choose my words, for as Joel Osteen stated, *"Your words have creative power. Whenever you speak something out, good or bad, you are giving life to what you are saying. Your words affect generations after you. Speak blessings and favor over them."*

After being laid off in 2009, I returned to college to finish what I started twenty years ago. I am currently in college, unemployed and on welfare, raising four children.

Though I try not to let my children see me worry about finances or know about our meager existence, at times it becomes disheartening to have to choose between buying your children a video game and/or a toy and paying a bill. However, the easiest way I can explain to my kids the choices I have to make is by sharing this scenario with them: I turn off the lights, the television, and anything electric. I follow up with closing the curtains and the room door. When they start to say, "Momma, it's dark,"

I proceed to tell them that if I don't pay the bills, that's what will happen and the difference is I won't be able to turn everything on by flicking a switch or pushing a button on the remote control. It may seem like a cruel and unusual way to teach a lesson, but it is one that each of them can completely understand. It is age appropriate and I'd rather show them in a hypothetical way, than for them to actually experience what it is like to be without electricity, water, or gas.

The understanding when they can't have everything they want and the appreciation when they get something that they ask for is priceless. I'm not saying my kids are perfect, because like all children do, they sometimes pout when things don't go their way. Nevertheless, I like to think that I have some extraordinary and remarkable children. When most children throw tantrums, complain and become rebellious, I am thankful that my children comprehend, respect, and accept the choices that I make.

I'm thankful for their appreciative and humble ways. I believe that God handpicked them *just* for me.

My motivation is being able to provide the basic necessities for them and sometimes giving them some of the things they want. I strive to instill in them good values and morals. We pray together as a family. Being a mother has been rewarding and fulfilling; coincidentally, being a mom has strengthened my faith in God.

Lichol Ford is a mother of four children. She currently lives in Rosharon, Texas. She can be reached at licholf@yahoo.com.

Diary of a Depressed Mom
BY JAMESINA E. GREENE

When you are blessed to be a mother, you take on a twenty-four-hour, seven-day-a-week commitment. Motherhood does not provide for sick days, vacation days, or personal leave time wherein you can cease to be a mother. Your role as "mother" continues even in those moments when you are just not feeling it. There was a period in my life when it took every bit of my inner strength to even get up in the morning, much less be "Mom." Many mornings when I opened my eyes, I would lie in bed trying to think of reasons why I should get up. Inevitably, my children would be my No. 1 reason.

In 1995, I was diagnosed with a mental illness, specifically, major and clinical depression. During this period, I did not like or love myself very much, but strangely enough, I never stopped loving my children. At the time of my diagnosis, I was a single mother of two sons. In addition, I was working full time and attending college part time. Needless to say, I was living in a state of overwhelming stress and always on the emotional edge. Depression is an illness that affects the body, mood, and thoughts. Statistics show that twice as many women suffer with depression as men. It is also known to be the number one disability in women. Therefore, if you are a mother and are suffering with this debilitating disease, it stands to reason that your role as a mother will be affected. Just as with any other disease, depression must first be acknowledged and recognized so that it can be dealt with. Depression should be determined by a healthcare professional and treated accordingly.

In my life, the multiple roles that I was attempting to fulfill, were draining the very life out of me. But the one role that both frightened and intrigued me was the role of "mom." I am convinced that my children's' dependence on me is what led me to seeking and receiving the help that I needed. Our children are "gifts" and must be treated as such. No matter the circumstances of their births, they are gifts.

Children give a mother a sense of purpose and focus for her life. We have the privilege and responsibility to mold them, guide them, and love them unconditionally. By doing so, we provide for them a safe place to land when life knocks them off of their feet.

The passion for motherhood will keep you going even when you feel like stopping. As a mother, especially battling depression, there are moments when you feel like you make wrong choices and bad decisions for your children. You often find yourself questioning relationships and motives. But the one thing for sure is that if you keep God in the center of your life and in the lives of your children, you will always get back on the right road.

Oftentimes, I would unexpectedly recall the indescribable love that I felt the first time I held them in my arms. As I looked into the eyes of each special gift, I was consumed with a power that made me feel as if I could conquer anything. When I allow myself to remember that feeling, I know that no mountain in my life is insurmountable, including depression.

I have learned through trial and error that the most important thing for me is not to just be a mother, but to be a "healthy" mother. The state of my health, physically, spiritually, and emotionally, greatly impacts the state of my children's health. I am the mother of princes and have the great privilege of raising them into the kings they were destined to be.

Today, I am a mother on a mission. I am the voice of my children, my grandchildren, and all of the children in my world. I have arrived at a place where I know how to unconditionally love my children and I am unconditionally loved by them. I am valued by my children and I value them as the individual gifts that they are.

Over the years, I have unofficially adopted many children and become "Mom" to them. I believe that my willingness to be real with them is what draws them to me. When you have a mother's heart, you automatically mother people, even if you did not give birth to them. Motherhood is the greatest assignment in the world and today, I can honestly say, I love it!

Jamesina E. Greene is the mother of two sons and the grandmother of four. She is an ordained minister, self-published author and resides in the state of Virginia.

Diary of a Stay-at-Home Mom

BY DEBORAH GAFFNEY

The Beginning...

My husband was finishing up his residency when we decided to start "practicing" to have our first baby. Of course, that practicing was the fun part. Most of our friends who were married and having children shared with us their stories regarding how long they "practiced" before they were blessed with a child. So, my ever logical, plan-everything husband suggested we start "practicing" six months prior to his finishing his residency. His theory was that it would take us a year to conceive. We would be settled in a new location and have double income for at least twelve months before our new bundle of joy arrived.

I visited with my ob/gyn and I was told that it would be difficult for me to conceive, but I wasn't worried with that news. We were in no hurry; we were just "practicing." I decided that I needed to be as healthy as possible, so I started taking vitamins religiously. I've always exercised and of course, I had stopped taking "the pill" in October.

In December, my husband decided to make the Christmas dinner. The Christmas duck was prepared with love by my husband, and I was pampered all day with spiked eggnog. It was a wonderful Christmas and our last Christmas with "Just the Two of Us."

Our first child was born in September of the following year, slightly ahead of our practice schedule. That's pretty much how we were blessed with each child. I would make a statement, "Let's start practicing for another child," and boom—baby! Well, nine months later, a baby.

I'll never forget that first moment I thought I might actually be pregnant. I had just received a promotion at work and life was fabulous! I had stopped at the store on the way home from work and picked up an EPT. I couldn't sleep that night, so I got up and tried out the test. After waiting an eternity for the test to develop, I jumped on the bed exclaiming, "It's blue; it's blue!!" It was 5 a.m. That's how my husband found out he was going to be a father.

Our firstborn was named after my mother, and my husband's grandmother. We had moved, two months prior to her birth, to another country. My husband was trying to grant me the wish of being a stay-at-home mom, so we moved from the East Coast, where I was born and raised, to the country of Texas. I know, it's not its own country anymore, but it once was and that pride still remains.

I've grown quite fond of the area, people, and the climate. You DO NOT KNOW LOVE until you have a child, born of love. She was perfect. She wouldn't nurse, wouldn't sleep for me (she'd sleep for her daddy), and she would occasionally spit up (as in rather forceful projectile spit up) after her meals, but she was perfect. I stayed at home with her, carried her, sang to her, and watched her grow. In fact, I carried her so much, she didn't learn to crawl until we went for a well check and the pediatrician asked if she had started trying to pull up. I calmly replied, "Pull up from where? I never put her down."

Needless to say, the pediatrician gently encouraged me to go home, clean whatever I thought needed to be cleaned so that I could put down a blanket and "…lay my child on the floor…" She actually smiled at me when she said it.

I asked her, "Why on earth would I lay my child on the floor?"

And she replied, "So that she can learn to roll over, pull up, learn to stand, and learn to crawl."

Well, laugh if you must, but after I got home, I placed our baby in her swing and I began to clean. I scrubbed the floors and baseboards. I dusted; I vacuumed; I mopped. I basically exhausted myself. Then I found a large blanket and laid it on the living room floor. I took our baby out of the swing and placed her in the center of the blanket. I grabbed my camera and waited... approximately five seconds. The child pushed up, rolled over, and laughed. Hmm, the doctor could have been right...this time.

I can't begin to tell you how many times I took that child's picture. And home movies! If I were organized enough to file everything appropriately...well, that would take too much time and I would miss out on her childhood. I did write in journals trying to chronicle everything so that when our baby was older, she could read about her childhood. Well, okay, the first year of her childhood. Because at the milestone of her first birthday, I suggested we try for a son. My husband agreed and nine months later, our son was born!

Two babies...how absolutely delightful. He was perfect. He had a cherub face, a gorgeous smile, and an infectious laugh. But realistically, how many of you can keep yourself from laughing if a baby starts to laugh?

Now I had two wonderful babies to take in my baby jogger around the neighborhood, to the Galleria, the zoo, and the Children's Museum. There's so much to see and do in our wonderful world. I wanted to share it all with them. We danced; we listened to all types of music; we sang, and we watched the cartoons that I had watched growing up. We had tea parties and went to the ballet. We played kickball and soccer and wiffle ball. We rode bikes and played tag and freeze tag. We organized and started a play group for all our neighborhood friends.

Our darling son was "all boy." He was the child who showed our daughter how to properly go down the slide, standing up and running. He was the child who defended his four-year-old sister from another four-year-old who was teasing her. He was two at the time and I was very pregnant with our third child, a darling little girl. Same scenario. Twelve months hit and I thought…baby!!

The third child was an interesting trip to the land of bed rest. I thought the ob/gyn had lost his mind when he said, "The baby is trying to come too soon and we are going to have to put you on complete bed rest."

I asked him to define "complete," and he actually opened his mouth and formed the words, "Don't do anything except go to the bathroom. If you have any contractions, call me. And if you can't follow instructions, I'll put you in the hospital."

I told him he didn't have to get all testy and I went home and started trying to prepare for baby number three. The preparation lasted approximately ten minutes, at which time I was hit with a massive contraction. The baby and I retired to the bed where we stayed for the next month, being entertained by the two little ones and the ever-present nanny. When I made the milestone of thirty-six weeks, my ob/gyn told me I could remove myself from bed rest.

It was Easter weekend and the neighborhood recreation committee was planning the annual Easter egg hunt. I missed the planning and organizing that year because of bed rest. But fresh from house arrest, I put my two babies in the jogger and I pushed them to the Easter egg hunt in the park. They found eggs and played with their friends. I reveled in being out of the house. We walked home and the two babies went outside to help their daddy wash his Corvette (hmm, that's another diary entry). Well, I was hit with a contraction from Hades—apparently my past due debt for making a child stay where she no longer wanted to be. Seriously, I had already had two children, the first by Caesarian and the second naturally, but never had I experienced such pain. I actually forgot how to breathe. My brain was trying to find a way to escape. The child wanted out. She had missed her first Easter egg hunt and she wasn't happy.

Looking back, I was quite terrified by the intensity of the contractions. I thought if I was extremely quiet my uterus might get tired and go to sleep. Yeah, didn't happen. So the third baby was born Easter Weekend.

That is the express version of how I became a stay-at-home mom to three wonderful babies. It has indeed been a delightful trip. They have shown me unconditional love, unconditional patience, and unconditional understanding. They have made me a more loving and complete person. They will always be my babies. They will always bring me joy.

Deborah Gaffney is the mother of three beautiful and talented children. She and her husband live in League City, Texas, where they have raised their children over the last twenty years. You can read more of her work at http://www.blogger.com/blogger. g?blogID=9045035166281251935#overview/src=dashboard

Diary of a Praying Mother

BY GINA JOHNSON

I am a praying mother. I am a stay-at-home-mother. I am a homeschooling mother. But I am a praying mother first. If I wasn't, I wouldn't have the strength to effectively raise my eight-year-old daughter, and my sons—ages four and nineteen months.

I begin each day in prayer. I end each day in prayer, and I take several breaks during the day to talk to God in prayer. Some may argue such redundant behavior isn't necessary, but I beg to differ. Communing closely with my Savior keeps me sane. Keeps me focused, and keeps me grateful every day for the incredible gift that my children are.

I wasn't always a praying mother, but as life happened, I quickly understood the behavior of my parents and grandparents, and became that much more grateful for their Godly example. I've had hardships turned into miracles. This is why I pray.

FEBRUARY 23, 2006

The downfall of the economy directly affected my blue-collar family. My husband's hours at work were drastically reduced, and we could barely buy groceries. I was tired of worrying constantly, so I began putting into practice years of sermons that I had heard my entire life. It was time to pray.

I woke up early on February 23rd. I remember the date vividly because it was my mother's birthday. I started my day in prayer.

Asked God to order my steps. Made an early trip to the grocery store, but I first decided to use the change in my car to treat myself to a cappuccino at our local coffee shop. As I drove in the direction of the coffee shop, God made it clear to me that I wasn't supposed to go. How did I know? I just did. God didn't speak to me audibly. He spoke in my spirit. In my heart. And I knew that I wasn't supposed to get a cappuccino that day. I was supposed to be at the grocery store. I reluctantly obeyed and made a U-turn to head back in the direction of the grocery store.

I needed to get groceries and make sure I had money left over to buy my mother a birthday card. As I strolled the aisles and filled my cart, I saw a cute, silver-haired Caucasian couple, who I imagine were in their seventies. I saw this same couple about three times during my grocery shopping trip. Every time I saw them, they smiled and exchanged pleasantries. I continued shopping and was almost finished when the elderly man approached me. His wife wasn't with him. He walked up to me and said, "The Lord told me to give you this."

He then handed me a twenty-dollar bill. Twenty dollars may not seem like a lot to most people, but at that time, twenty dollars meant a lot to me. I burst into tears and hugged the man.

"Every time I saw you, the Lord told me to give you the money. Three times, God told me to, but I didn't do it. So on our way out the door, I told my wife: 'Honey, God told me to give that young lady some money.' My wife said, 'Then go find her and give it to her!'"

That event changed my life. How awesome to know that the God of the Universe had me on His mind that morning! So much so that He allowed someone else to bless me. Had I gotten the cappuccino, I wouldn't have been at the grocery store at that time. The place of blessing. I probably would never have seen the elderly couple. I'm so glad I prayed that morning. It put me in tune with God. I heard Him that morning when He told me not to get the cappuccino. Had I been disobedient and gone to the coffee shop anyway, I would've missed an incredible blessing. This is why I pray.

DECEMBER 2006

"I'm having fun, Mommy!" My three-year-old daughter giggled as she climbed into bed between my husband and me.

My eyes were reunited with familiar tears as I tied Cierra's scarf around her neck, and helped her put her mittens on. My husband and I avoided eye contact as he covered me and Cierra with blanket after blanket, doing his best to keep us warm. I knew if I looked into his eyes at that moment, those familiar sad tears, that seemed to frequent my eyes quite often, would flow like a river. I couldn't let Cierra see that. She had no idea that the hearts of her parents were extremely heavy.

After the last blanket was added, my husband, Karl, put on his coat and gloves and climbed into bed.

Cierra's mahogany cheeks were accented with rosiness ushered in by the cold.

"Mommy, I'm kinda cold." Cierra laughed, nestling herself deeper into the mountain of blankets, sheets, and comforters.

"I know, baby," I whispered, as I wiped the tears from my cold face.

It has to get better, I thought. We can't go an entire winter with no heat.

Karl and I wrapped our arms around Cierra and she soon fell fast asleep. She was warm, and we were relieved.

As I lay there comforted by the warmth of our three bodies snuggled closely, I whispered a prayer to God. It was all I could do at that moment, and God comforted me. Helped me to get a good night's sleep in what was an intense trial for our family.

My husband was out of work. Our car had been repossessed. We were on the verge of losing everything. We hadn't told our families that we didn't have any heat. We didn't really see the purpose in doing so. It would only make them worry and none of our relatives were wealthy enough to pay the excessive bill.

Living in poverty with no heat, certainly wasn't how I imagined my life would be when I had married my husband seven years prior. But job loss and a broken economy contributed heavily to our family's misfortunes. With gas prices soaring, it was nearly impossible to keep up with the cost of our heating bill. Back in April, we knew that our gas would be shut off, but in the spring, we had no need for heat. We had to pay our electric bill and our gas bill, but only had the cash to pay one or the other. We could survive in the spring without heat, but not without electricity, so we opted to keep our electricity on, in hopes of our financial situation improving by fall when outside temperatures would start dropping again. What we didn't plan on was my husband not being able to find steady work. Winter was swiftly approaching and we didn't have heat. Not only was our gas bill sky high, but the gas company had been adding late fees for every month that we didn't pay. We contacted several charitable organizations seeking help, but no one was able to help us. Our small town only had a few agencies that assisted the poor and they had already been bombarded by others also seeking help.

My heart was so heavy. Prayer was the only thing that sustained me. I prayed constantly. Told God how I felt. Listened to Him tell me it was going to be all right. I remember being surprised that God hadn't intervened and worked something out for us so that our heat would be turned on before winter. I learned something else instead. God will sometimes allow us to go through extreme hardships in order to strengthen our faith and motivate us to pray like never before. My prayers became fervent. I prayed for God's provisions. We needed money and lots of it. I prayed for God's protection. We needed safety because unfortunately, we had to use space heaters and the oven to keep our house warm. The only time we turned all of our heating devices off was when we had to be away from our home for extended periods of time. Then and only then, would we turn the oven and space heaters off. When we returned home, our house would be a refrigerator and we would have to put on layers of clothing and snuggle up together in bed until our house grew warm once again. But I prayed. I wouldn't stop praying and I wouldn't stop believing that things would get better.

Fast-forward a few months. My husband had a steady job, and we were struggling to get back on our feet, but the gas bill still haunted us. I was eight months' pregnant with our second child that we definitely had not planned on. Our gas bill had been plagued with late fees for over a year and was now a whopping $3,000. I feared that our newborn, expected to join us in September, would be in harm's way if he lived in a home that didn't have heat during a harsh Michigan winter.

One day, a friend of mine called me to see how my pregnancy was going. We began chatting about our faith in God, and for some reason, I told her our secret. That we didn't have any heat, and hadn't had heat in about eighteen months. I had been in this bad situation for so long that I no longer realized how horrible it really was, but from the outside looking in, it was alarming. My girlfriend cried. I told her not to worry because we weren't. We had already survived one winter, and we knew God would provide before the next winter. About a week later, my girlfriend called back.

"Gina, when you told me you had no heat, I couldn't sleep that night."

"I shouldn't have told you. I didn't want you to worry," I lamented.

"Well, I hope you don't mind, but at Bible Study, I asked my church to pray for a needy family who didn't have heat last winter, and feared that they wouldn't have heat this upcoming winter. I didn't give them your names."

My heart smiled.

"Thanks for having them pray for us! That really means a lot."

"There's more, Gina. After church, a woman approached me and asked me how much your bill was."

My cheeks grew warm with embarrassment. I didn't want to tell her that we owed $3,000. Before I could get a word out, my friend continued.

"We called the gas company and...well, long story short, your bill has been paid in full."

All I could do was cry and thank God. A couple, whom I had never seen, paid our gas bill in its entirety. Over $3,000. Paid in full. God had answered my prayer.

This is why I pray.

MAY 18, 2010

It was a busy morning. Cierra was going to be late for her swim class if we didn't hurry.

"Come on! We've got to go!" I shouted.

Cierra scurried out the door as I picked up my eighteen-month-old and slung him on my hip.

We jumped in the van and headed toward the highway. My children were singing and I was distracted. The only thing on my mind was that we needed to HURRY! I approached a busy intersection that allowed for right turns during a red light. The next couple of seconds are a blur. I think I looked both ways before I turned, but I honestly can't remember. All I remember is turning the corner and then *CRASH*!

We were briefly in the air before the impact on the grassy knoll. I was instantly in pain, but tried my best to maneuver our van in such a way to prevent it from flipping. After what seemed like forever, our van came to a stop.

My children were screaming. I turned to the right and could see my son, Tré, still strapped into his car seat. I attempted to turn around to check on my daughter who was directly behind me, but I couldn't. The pain was too great. I could see her in the rearview mirror and was alarmed at the sight of blood on her forehead.

That's when I heard the sirens. Several ambulances and at least one fire truck. My memory of the details surrounding the accident are still somewhat blurry.

The jaws of life were used to remove me from the vehicle. I remained calm for my hysterical children. I kept smiling through the tears, and reassuring them through the pain. "We're fine. It's all right."

A kind stranger dialed my husband's number and held the phone to my ear. I was in too much pain to do so myself. I was so calm while informing Karl about the accident, that he thought it was only a fender-bender. He later told me that when he got to the accident scene, it looked like something out of a movie. The expression on his face told me that things were far more severe than I realized.

Throughout that day, several people—the paramedics, nurses, and doctors—told me how lucky we were. I was sure to correct them. We weren't lucky, we were blessed. After all, I only suffered a broken shoulder blade along with a few torn muscles and ligaments. Cierra had a few cuts on her forehead, and Tré was completely unharmed. It wasn't until I was released from the hospital that night that I found out what hit us: a semi-truck carrying a 200,000-pound bulldozer. It wasn't just a blessing that we were all right. It was a miracle. Someone should've died, but God saw fit to protect us.

About two weeks later, I got the shock of my life when I found out that I was pregnant. All I could think of was the fact that I'd had a CAT scan on the day of the accident, and I had been taking Vicodin for the pain in my shoulder. Before I had the CAT scan, I was asked over and over if there was a chance that I could be pregnant. I thought about it for a minute. I'm a married woman. There's always a "chance." But I highly doubted it, so I went on and had the CAT scan. After finding out that I was pregnant, I researched the risks involved with taking strong meds, and even worse, the risks involved with having a CAT scan while pregnant. Developmental problems and heart complications were only a couple of the risks that my unborn child faced.

There was nothing I could do but pray.

I spent the rest of my pregnancy praying that my child would be 100 percent healthy. On January 28, 2011, God answered my prayer when our ten-pound, one-ounce son, Joshua, entered the world. Joshua means "God saves" and we knew that name was more than appropriate for him.

Those are only three examples of what God has done in my life as a result of being a praying mother.

Through it all, I pray. If I need wisdom in rearing my children, I pray. If I need wisdom in being a wife, I pray. If I need help finding my keys, I pray. I have learned to give everything to God. The insignificant as well as the significant. I'm not a perfect mother. I'm a praying mother. I have peace. I have happiness. I have joy, and I can smile—even when life's forecast is stormy.

This is why I pray.

Gina Johnson is an aspiring author. She lives in Southwest Michigan with her husband of twelve years and their three children.

Diary of an Unemployed Mom
BY ROISHINA CLAY HENDERSON

Over the last few months, I have laid my head down on tear-stained pillows from crying myself to sleep many nights in wrestling with that demon called Depression. Thankfully, God's peace has arrested and rescued my spirit many times from sliding downhill into a state of hopelessness. My young son has also been a saving grace in helping me to maintain my sanity while being unemployed. I feel as though I am that "stay-at-home mom…by force."

I don't mean being a stay-at-home mom by force as a negative connotation, but it's a reality. My reality. When you're accustomed to working and desire to have a career outside of the home life, it's a crippling challenge to adapt to being a stay-at-home mom—especially for an extended period of time. It doesn't take away that I have a ton of respect for mothers who make the decision to be homemakers or happily choose the path of being a stay-at-home mom; it is indeed work and many times harder work with fewer praises. It's rewarding, but nonetheless, it's still work.

The downward spiral of the job economy hasn't lifted in my experience as of yet. I have suffered not one but three job casualties in the past few years. So it's been a shocking, painful blow to the spirit when one loves to have a career but can't find it—as I'm sure many others can also testify to. To suffer job losses, it's a hurting, humbling feeling that I'm still dealing with. As a mother, I always want to provide the best possible life I can for my son.

And into today's world, there's no getting around it that it helps to have the proper finances in place to be able to do the things you want to for your family. The mounting bills and buying life's necessities don't cease just because you've lost your job.

Though this is where the gleams of light come in for me. Being a divorced, stay-at-home mom has afforded me some priceless pleasures that I'm sure most working moms would kill for: the time to take my son to school each morning and see his handsome face when school lets out in the early afternoons rather than waiting until the evening news is about to go off when we would both be tired from a long day.

I could've been drowning in my sorrows or the frustrations of another job rejection just moments before it's time to pick him up from school. However, I've always managed to put on the biggest smile and ask, "How was your day, Sweet Face?"

I eagerly await his routine response, which on most days is "good." And then he goes into his spiel of how he was a good boy and wants to be rewarded with having time to play games on the computer or going out to dinner.

He never sees my tears, but he understands when I tell him there's not enough money in the stretched budget at the moment for dinner at one of his favorite restaurants. Still, he curls up under my arms, leaving no room for space between him and me. His mere presence eases the temporary hurt that I battle over being unemployed for so long.

But when he's fast asleep in the middle of the night, it feels like a dark cloud hovers over me sometimes and penetrates my emotions. I find myself on the computer as late as two and three o'clock in the morning almost every night sending my resume to tons of companies. I'm hoping and wishing to get a call back for an opportunity to get back into the work force that I once found so much fault in. It's funny how you miss those things you once complained so much about when they're taken away from you.

I'm not sure what life's lesson is going to come out of this, but I know it's not in vain while I'm in this holding pattern. I still choose to look at the brighter picture of being a stay-at-home mom, and treasuring the times I get to have with my son—something I didn't have as much in his toddler years. He's seven years old now and growing at an accelerated rate—mentally, emotionally, and definitely physically as he's already eating me out of house and home.

I had a career in public relations, where it wasn't uncommon for me to work long hours. In my last job, it was routine for me to make it home after six-thirty or seven o'clock in the evenings.

Now that I've been out of work for a year, I get those hours back with my son. And I'm able to spend quality time with him, rather than fixing a quick dinner, doing homework, making sure he gets his bath and brushes his teeth, ironing school uniforms and then sending him straight to bed on the weekdays. Where was the quality time in that?

On Mondays, we completely finish an entire week's worth of homework on that one day, so we can hang out—just the two of us—during the rest of the week. Now I have those long talks with my son. I'm able to watch him play and run around. We leisurely go the grocery store as he grabs his favorite fruits and snacks. But best of all, I can snuggle with him on the couch as we watch TV, as I inhale his distinctive scent, rub his soft, warm cheeks against my face until he gets tired of me and squirms out of my reach. I relish in this time of being able to have him in my arms before he reaches the pre-teen and teen years of possibly not wanting me to love on him as much as I do now with all the hugs and kisses.

Last summer will be one for me to always remember. It was the first time I had the chance to be at home the entire summer and maximize the time with my son. His father and I chose not to go the summer camp route. But instead, my son and I did fun, weekly activities to get out the house and enjoy the summer with trips to the recreation center to get in the pool, trips to downtown Atlanta to act as tourists, and being involved in our church's student summer feeding program. We also made a trip back to my parents' home in Mississippi, where he enjoyed time with the grandparents and his cousins whom he doesn't see often.

Though not working and not having the income I desire weighs heavily on me at times, I find joy in just hanging with my baby who is totally unaware of his mother's worries of not finding work.

God is still working on me, as I discover and finally secure my calling in life. I have a hunch of what it is. But I think God has routed me in this direction to pay attention to something that's way more important than any career could ever offer, and that's being the best possible mother I can be to my son and to not miss out on some the most critical, potential-for-molding opportunities a mother could ask for. Could I still witness these great moments of watching my son grow up or still wear the "S" on my chest as a full-time working mother? Absolutely yes. But in God's infinite wisdom, He saw fit for me to take time out right now to be a stay-at-home mother.

While I'm working on being an *even better* mother, I'm still working on being a better me and learning to accept life's challenges. So my life is a work in progress. Life's joys and setbacks won't end here. But in the next chapters of life, I feel I will be better equipped to handle what is thrown my way—be it good or bad.

I'm not so sure I would've escaped severe depression had it not been for being a mom to that wonderful little man I have in my life. I think God places things and people in our lives at the right times to teach us, help us, and sustain us. He's got our lives totally mapped out. Unknowingly, my son has helped me in all those ways, and I'm a better mom for it.

Roishina Clay Henderson is a proud mother of one son. A Mississippi native, this former journalist is a graduate of Jackson State University and lives in Atlanta, Georgia. She is working on her second novel. Check out her website at www.roishina.com.

Diary of a Mature Mom
BY SHELBY ALEXANDER GRIGGS

As long as I can remember, I've always wanted to be a mother. My husband and I met in college, dated for three-and-a-half years and then got married. By then, we were in our late twenties and hopeful for the future. We wanted children eventually but wanted the luxury of choosing when that time came. I had just started my career and it became my number one focus. Two-and-a-half years later, I found out I was pregnant. The pregnancy came with many struggles, but I was blessed to give birth to my son, whom we named Johnathon. He was just the way I imagined him to be. He was mild-mannered, slept all night at six weeks old, and hardly ever cried. I continued to focus on my career and began to receive promotions to higher-level positions.

We talked about having another child when Johnathon was about five years old, but it never seemed to be a good time. Several years later, my management role had stabilized and we felt that we were ready to expand our family. I figured it would be easy because it had taken me less than six months to get pregnant with my son. After trying for more than six months, I finally got pregnant. If you're doing the math, you know that I was now in my thirties. Sadly, the pregnancy didn't last and I miscarried at eight weeks. Doctors told me it was normal to miscarry and that I was physically fine and could try again. Unfortunately, they were wrong. Little did I know, this would be the beginning of an emotional roller coaster filled with hope, then disappointment. From that point on, I had multiple losses and meanwhile was getting older and older.

I was fast approaching the big 4-0. I told my husband that if I had not gotten pregnant by then, all bets were off. I couldn't see myself having a baby at the age of forty-plus. To add to the situation, I really could not go through another loss. All of the pregnancies ended early, but they were still losses that caused a sea of emotions every time it happened. My son was growing into a teenager and it seemed impossible for me to think I could be a mother again, so I gave up the dream of having a daughter whom I could take shopping. My fortieth birthday had come and gone and I had made absolute peace with God's plan for me. When I said the words out loud, I was then able to truly accept it and move forward.

It was almost a year-and-a-half after my fortieth birthday celebration when I visited my sister who had just given birth to my little nephew and she was forty-one years old! I was there to help her but was extremely fatigued the entire weekend. I returned home Sunday night preparing for my week when I realized my period was late. Could it be? *Oh no, I'm not going there again*, I thought. I couldn't get it out of my mind, so I got a pregnancy test. It said positive. I quickly put it in a drawer and waited for my husband to come home. I didn't want to believe it. I'm sure you can guess how our conversation went.

"I'm pregnant."

"No, you're not."

"Yes, I am."

I wish I could tell you that this pregnancy happened without complications and drama, but I can't. What I will say is that once I got the final word that at forty-two years of age, I was going to have a baby, it was all good from there.

On December 22, 2009, I became a mother of a newborn baby girl named Mikayla. My son was fifteen. I was really okay with not having another child and certainly never believed that I could have one at forty-two years old after all of the losses I'd had.

People often ask me if parenting in my forties is different from when I was parenting my son in my twenties and I say YES! The world is different and the images on TV, in magazines, even the cartoons, are different. The media is very risqué and I'm finding that I have to keep a lot more from Mikayla than I did with Johnathon. Even the animated shows and movies are over the top. It's irritating to know that so much is out in the world and I'm trying. I know Mikayla will be exposed to these things at some point, but I want to delay that exposure as long as possible. My mother used to tell me when I was a teenager, and getting on her nerves, that one day I was going to get back the attitude I gave her. I believed that I had dodged that bullet because Johnathon was so easygoing as a child and even as a teen. He never gave me trouble, and he usually walked the straight and narrow. Mikayla, on the other hand, is bossy, talks back, has tantrums, and laughs when I give her the "I wish you would" stare. With all that wrapped up in her personality, she's a girl. We girls know drama and mine gives me plenty! My mother is grinning ear to ear at the moment.

Although Johnathon was pretty much a mild-mannered child, he still challenged me in other ways. He was always honest to a fault. I remember one Saturday morning, we were having breakfast at a local buffet restaurant. Johnathon's classmate walked up to the table to say hello and my son wanted to know where his parents were. When the little boy said they were going back to the buffet for seconds, Johnathon told him his parents were going to be fat. My husband almost choked from laughter.

Johnathon also had an opportunity to meet the Dallas Cowboys cheerleaders and when they asked for his name so that they could give him their autograph, he politely told them that their uniforms were too small and that they needed to buy new ones. I spent a lot of time explaining to Johnathon what not to say in public. Sometimes it worked and sometimes it didn't.

Case in point, a man in the grocery store line spoke to him and smiled. He was wearing braces and Johnathon asked him if he didn't think he was too old for braces. I'm telling you, I can't make this stuff up!

Johnathon's willingness to speak his mind was often brutally honest, but it was helpful in raising him. My parents always said that there was no book to tell them how to be parents and they just winged it based on how they were raised. I understand that now. I have done the same, but I've also paid attention to my children's personalities. Johnathon always responded to words, so I didn't have to spank him much, but we talked to him often. I remember when he was eight years old, he called a family meeting. He asked my husband and me to sit down because he had something important to say. The funny thing was that while we sat, he stood up and he began what we call the John Willy revival. He shared his concerns about school; then he discussed our parenting methods. We were not allowed to speak and he commenced giving us the run-down. His topics of discussion ranged from disciplinary methods to his opinion of how we were treating one another. It was always important for Johnathon to have a safe place to share his thoughts, good or bad.

I grew up in a strict military home. My dad was extremely rigid and although my mother was firm, she was a good balance for us. She sometimes allowed us to negotiate things. We had the talks and the old school whippings with the belt; that's just how it was back then. However, we did also have family discussion time that took place at least once a month. It was our time to sit down with our parents and talk about what was on our minds. We talked about everything from the classes we were struggling with in school to the boy we had a crush on. My mother said that little did we know that they were trying to figure out what we were up to. I was the oldest with the biggest mouth. My parents didn't have to work hard to get information out of me. My sister, on the other hand, locked her business up like Fort Knox. She challenged my parents often, especially my father.

Raising children with all of the present technology is much more difficult. You have the technology piece, which can be a plus but can also create a huge challenge in keeping up with your kids. I didn't buy my son a cell phone until he was in middle school, which was a bit early, but he was in school activities and staying after school. It was more about peace of mind for me. Of course, back in my day, cell phones weren't available and all you had was your house phone and the pay phone. I didn't get a phone in my room until my senior year in high school. Before that, my parents were answering the phone and forbidding me to talk on it after 9 p.m. I shared a phone line with the household and anyone could pick up an extension and listen to my calls, which my parents often did.

Today, teenagers have the cell phones, but they don't really talk on them. I don't think I've ever heard my son talk to anyone on his phone. Instead, he is texting from sun-up to sundown. I also noticed that he started to lock his phone so I politely asked for the combination. One day, he walked up on my reading his text messages and asked me what I was doing. I replied, "Parenting." I also told him that since his father worked for the cell phone carrier, we could get access to his messages even if he deleted them so don't bother. I'm especially proud of that one, even though it wasn't exactly the truth. I check backpacks, drawers, closets, you name it. This is the way you parent in the New Millennium.

Facebook came along and gave me another thing to police. After a while, I mellowed out and allowed Johnathon to get a page—if I was accepted as his friend. For the most part, he kept it pretty clean. I learned that if I wanted to connect with him, I had to know the music he was listening to, the teen lingo, and now the texting acronyms. With the racial climate in America, we felt that it was imperative that our son was taught about inter-racial relationships and being a black male in predominantly white suburbia. The most challenging thing was getting him to understand that despite his respectful demeanor, some girl's father was not going to like him with her simply because of the color of his skin. Unfortunately, he had to learn the hard way and we talked through it and other racial encounters he had, and encouraged him not to be bitter but to be wiser from it.

Many parents think that if they get engaged with their kids, especially teens, the kids lose respect for them. I'm not talking about twisting open a beer and shooting the breeze, but I do believe that we have to entertain the conversations of our children to stay connected to them. I never wanted my son to say that he felt he couldn't come to us because we either wouldn't listen or we wouldn't understand. Johnathon loves hip-hop dancing and rapping. Do you know how many dance combinations I've watched? How many rap songs I've heard? I would be in the middle of writing a chapter for my book, and I would have to put it down to watch a dance routine he memorized from a Chris Brown video. My husband is doing the same, but he takes it up one notch; he uses some of the lingo and my son thinks he's the coolest dad ever! It keeps us engaged, and no matter how painful it can be at times, he knows that we are the parents, but we care about what he's interested in. Not to mention, we are aware of what's going on with him as well.

Oh, my darling little Mikayla. Unfortunately for her, I'm a wiser and a premenopausal mother with zero tolerance for whining. Despite her feisty personality, we still enjoy each other. Some days I look at her and can't believe she is here. I have this little girl who looks like me and loves "sparkly" things, as she says, just like her mama. I often hear people say that she's so smart, she "has been here before." I'm not sure if it's that or the fact that I'm talking more and that she has nothing but older people around her. Mikayla was saying words clearly at eight months, so we could see that she was going to be a talker. I will say that in this day and age, it's hard to censor things from her. If I don't have *Sesame Street* on the television 24/7, she's bound to pick up something from a commercial or a TV show.

I want to share with you a funny story about how much my daughter is a sponge. I was watching one of Tyler Perry's *Madea* plays and Mikayla was in the room playing. Two days later, she says to Johnathon, "Madea says, go to hell." I almost lost it. With all of the biblical references in the play, that was the one thing she remembered. So, I had to pull *Madea* from my viewing list at least while she was around. It's even harder to handle her when she comes back from daycare. Mikayla attends a school with a small number of minority kids in her class right now, and I'm not trying to offend folks, but she is picking up some serious drama scenes from Becky and Megan.

When I was growing up, telling your mother to be quiet was followed by a pop across the mouth. Mikayla is two years old now, but I pop those legs because she comes home and tries all of that nonsense on me. I do see many similarities between her and Johnathon. Mikayla is very affectionate like him, a talker, and most of all wants to please people. With her strong personality, it has kept me young and has required me to be much more on my toes.

Having children in your forties has its advantages and disadvantages. As I'm writing this, I am forty-four years old with a birthday coming up next week, which makes me excited and thankful. The truth about having a toddler at my age, it confuses people about my real age. I was talking to a parent in Mikayla's class and she was telling me that I should give her another sibling. I told her that it was out of the question. She kept pushing until I finally said, "Look, Lady, I'm in my forties. This factory is closed!"

Johnathon hates to go to the mall with me. I'm always asking him to help me with her, and he says that he hates to because people think she's his. So, as silly as it sounds, if I see a girl I think he's trying to impress, I won't call his name, but call him "Son." Hollywood makes motherhood in your forties look so very chic. Well, pump the brakes on that! What women need to know is those Hollywood women have nannies to handle the snotty noses and trainers to get rid of that belly fat that has set up shop in your mid-section. Don't get me started with all of the hormonal changes that come with this age bracket. You have to know how excited I was when I heard Doctor Oz say that peri-menopausal rage was normal.

With that said, being an older mom has its challenges, but I wouldn't trade the experience for the world. I see it as my second act, my second chance to fine-tune my mothering skills. At the end of the day, I'm thankful to have been blessed with my dream as a young girl and that was to have my son first, my girl second. Doing so fifteen years apart wasn't a part of my plan, but if you want to make God laugh, tell him your plans.

Shelby has been married twenty years and is the mother of two children, Johnathon, 18, and Mikayla, 3. She lives in the northern suburb of Dallas, Texas, where she is a life coach, author, and motivational speaker. For more information, visit www.shelbyalexandergriggs.com

Diary of a Mom Trying to Conceive

BY FELICIA WILLIAMS

Every time I hear a news headline about abandoned, discarded, or abused children, I mutter some not-so-nice words about the ungrateful parents or guardians, and then quickly turn the channel.

Every time I heard a woman lamenting about her pregnancy, I turn and abruptly walk away. That's because for the longest, seeing that would cause an anger inside of me that I cannot even describe. Hearing the stories or listening to complaints was like a knife in my heart. After all, they had what I wanted. Children.

The road to becoming a mother has been the longest and, at times, the darkest road I have ever traveled in my life. Along my journey, I became an angry, bitter woman who obsessed about trying to get a home pregnancy test to show a positive sign and resented those around me who didn't have to work as hard to even become pregnant.

That was then. This is now.

I now appreciate my journey. It has made me a better mom.

I love being a mom and being able to see and nurture the gifts that God so graciously loaned me. Sure, sometimes I want Calgon to take me away and leave me on a remote island. And yes, at times, tears have been shed out of pure, unadulterated frustration during a homework session, but in the end, I wouldn't give it up for anything because the road to get here was full of peaks and valleys.

In 2001, a reproductive endocrinologist diagnosed me with

polycystic ovarian syndrome (PCOS). In a nutshell, my hormones were (and still are) out of whack, literally. Instead of my ovaries producing follicles, they produce cysts. This is important because no follicle = no egg. Since the cysts stay around for months on end, you end up with what is known as a "string of pearls" on your ovaries, and those pearls are not the kind any woman would want.

I didn't fit the "norm" of a PCOSer (I was thin and relatively healthy.) I just knew that this syndrome wasn't going to stand in my way of getting pregnant. I took Clomid (a relatively cheap drug used to promote ovulation and treat infertility) on my specified cycle days. We "did the deed" on the designated day, and then I peed on a stick ten days later.

BAM! I got my positive! It only took me two months of drugs to get pregnant!

Aside from some little molehills (partial placenta previa and gestational diabetes), I had a good pregnancy. I taught high school and coached cheerleading through my entire pregnancy, and in 2003 my husband and I welcomed our son, Ayinde, which means: we prayed to God and he came.

Looking back now, I am amazed at how quickly God chose to answer that prayer. Little did we know, it would be a long time before our prayer would be answered again.

In 2005, when our oldest was two, we started trying to conceive again. We had moved to Houston and I remember my new ob/gyn telling me that I was lucky to have even gotten pregnant the first time, given my history. Lucky? Hello?! Not the "typical cyster" here; thin, relatively healthy, first son only took two months to conceive. These doctors didn't know what they were talking about. Number two wouldn't be a problem, either!

Since Clomid worked so quickly before, we started with it again. After months of taking Clomid, and a few other medicines, under the care of that ob/gyn *and* a new RE, it was obvious that child number two was not going to happen as easily as it had for number one. Having to go to the doctor for bloodwork, taking pills at the same time on specific days, and "doing the deed" at the right time put me in the front seat of the TTC (trying to conceive) emotional roller coaster. I became stressed, frustrated, and spent. My dream, and plan, of perfectly spaced siblings was a bust.

We moved in 2006 and once we found our groove in the new city, we decided to try again. I found an ob/gyn and decided to give Clomid another shot, but this time we added a HCG shot (also known as a trigger shot) and progesterone. The Clomid helped me produce follicles, the trigger shot made sure the follicle ruptured so the egg would be released, and the supplemental progesterone provided the nourishment a "sticky" embryo might need to survive. That combination worked and I got pregnant in 2007. The kids wouldn't be two years apart; they'd be three years apart and that was fine with me.

Unfortunately, the three-year gap didn't matter because those dreams came to an end on a Tuesday afternoon when I was twelve weeks' pregnant. Since the progesterone's only job is to bridge the gap between the news of the BFP (big fat pregnancy) and the placenta forming, I stopped taking it at the end of my eleventh week. I miscarried three days later. The ultrasound showed that the baby had stopped developing at nine weeks, and the continued use of the progesterone only delayed the inevitable. I had just had an ultrasound at the beginning of my ninth week, and I had seen a dancing baby on the screen. I could see the arm and leg buds forming. I even brought the ultrasound pictures home to show my husband. It was devastating to know that at some point during that week, the baby stopped dancing. It just stopped. The loss was all encompassing. The physical pain was unlike anything

I had ever experienced, but the worst pain came when I had to explain to my four-year-old that there was no longer a baby in my tummy. That was one of the hardest things I've ever had to do.

Soon after the miscarriage I realized I needed a new ob/gyn. The doctor who I had been seeing wanted to argue about my PCOS diagnosis and refused to treat me as a PCOS patient, thus denying me the treatments or medicines that might help me conceive. After dealing with all of it, I also realized I needed a break. I had to deal with my loss and work on becoming my own health advocate. I found a therapist who specialized in women's issues (who knew they even existed), a psychologist to prescribe anti-depressants until the fog of depression lifted, and a new RE, the only doctor who truly knows the "ins and outs" of what can help a woman become pregnant. I was on a mission to find a doctor who was going to listen to me and what I knew to be true about my body; after all, I knew my body better than anyone.

I learned relatively quickly I had to go up a notch as far as drugs were concerned if I wanted a chance to become pregnant again. Time was not on my side because I sure wasn't getting any younger. So I switched to injections. This time I took shots to stimulate the ovaries, kept the trigger and progesterone, and added a baby aspirin for a clotting disorder that had been discovered. All the shots were given in my stomach, thigh, or butt. The location of the shots depended on which drug I was taking, the day, and how bad I had bruised from the previous night's shot. On top of that, I would go to the doctor's office every other day (including weekends) to get my blood drawn and have ultrasounds done; then I would wait for the afternoon call to tell me what changes to make for that evening's protocol. Driving back and forth in rush-hour traffic was a pain; trying to hide huge bruises on my forearms was, at times, a task, but I wanted a baby. I followed this protocol for months, and each month we got a big fat no, so we would make a few changes to increase our chance on the next cycle. Some months we did timed intercourse (that sounds fun and spontaneous, right?) and other months, we chose to do IUI (intrauterine insemination). An IUI is when the doctor takes the sperm, washes it to get rid of extra debris and bad "spermies," and spins it down to make it concentrated. That concentrated specimen is then inserted directly into the uterus. Of course, the idea is that since only super "spermies" remain, the chance of a "good one" finding its way to the egg is increased. The reality was that adding the IUI only increased our chances by maybe 7 percent, but that was 7 percent closer to a BFP. After each IUI, I would lie on a slightly, slanted exam table, so my head was closer to the floor than my feet for fifteen to twenty minutes, so gravity could help the "spermies" find their way. I'm telling you, we tried just about everything to make these infertility treatments a success, and I was willing to do whatever I needed to make it happen. Soon, though, it was obvious that we had to make a decision. It was time to either stop trying for another child altogether or move on to in vitro fertilization. The biological clock was sounding an alarm...so we switched doctors, again, and forged ahead this time using IVF. Initially, I did the IVF because my husband asked me to; after all, the task of shooting one's self in the stomach for days on end did not sound fun. In fact, on my first injection cycle, I "stimmed" (stimulated) for twelve days only to end up with ovaries the size of golf balls and a canceled cycle because I was overstimulated! It sucked!

The IVF protocol was like clockwork. I took pills to prepare my body, shots to stimulate the ovaries, a shot to prevent ovulation, antibiotics to prevent infection during the retrieval, and two kinds of progesterone two times per day to help in case we got a

BFP. The RE was able to retrieve twenty-nine eggs. Out of the twenty-nine, twenty-six were mature, and out of those fifteen fertilized "naturally" (meaning millions of "spermies" were put in a Petri dish with each egg and nature did its thing). The "embabies" were left to grow and after five days, nine good embryos remained. The question then became: how many do we transfer? Of course the thought is: the more transferred, the higher chance of getting a BFP. But, the RE only allowed us to transfer one embryo and freeze the rest. That "fresh" transfer of one perfect embryo was a success! It was 2010 and I was finally pregnant again!

Unfortunately, it was like déjà vu. In May 2010, almost three years to the day of my first loss, I found out that this baby had died as well. Could I not get a break? I seemed to be surrounded by "accidental pregnancies" or reading about people who should have never been allowed to be a mother or father in the first place, and here I was being a human pin cushion just to get an egg to appear! The shots, the hormones, pregnant women, miscarriages… all of it was pissing me off. It was even more frustrating because most of those around me couldn't understand or relate to *any* of what I had been through. In fact, only my husband, my best friend, Tara, and other "cysters" knew about the entire journey and the pregnancy. My husband had told his parents around eight weeks only for us to tell them two weeks later, we miscarried. Let me tell you, miscarriage and infertility are two topics that can silence a room, and I felt trapped in a huge room of silence.

After a few months of dealing with the second loss and praying for a peace that surpassed all understanding, I was ready to use those eight "embabies" that were on ice. In the fall of 2010, we transferred two and got a no two weeks later. I took another mental and emotional break and decided to try one last time in January 2011. This was going to be my last transfer. I was going to be thirty-eight that summer, and we were moving away. I was emotionally and physically drained, and I was too through with the financial aspect of all of this.

I put all my cards on the table. I wanted to transfer three embryos. Of course, I had to once again prepare my body with pills and shots.

Since this was the last hurrah, I was going to do all that I could here on earth to make it happen. This time, however, when I would do various parts of the regimen, I said this prayer: "Lord, whatever happens, happens. I am going to be thankful for my son, and I pray for peace no matter what the outcome."

Looking back at all of those previous cycles, I realized I never really had a sense of peace; I had anxiousness that I carried every single day in the pit of my stomach. But I can say that during that last attempt, I truly had peace. I was okay with having one child, and I was okay with the money we had spent on trying to have another. The fact of the matter was I had no right to complain because many, many "cysters" haven't been blessed with one child. Instead of focusing on what I didn't have, I had to shift my focus to what I already had.

So when I have those moments when I am looking up at the sky and counting to ten, I try to pause and remember: God has blessed me with so much more than I deserve and so much more than what others have. He allowed me to experience motherhood, not just once but a second time with the arrival of Ajani, whose name means: he who wins the struggle.

And what a struggle it was, but I wouldn't change a thing.

Felicia Williams lives in Indianapolis, IN with her husband and two boys.

Diary of a Struggling Mom
BY KIMYATTA WALKER

Today is Monday. I just spent my last ten dollars on a school fundraiser so that my daughter could have a chance to go to a bike show at her school. Payday is not until Friday. My gas tank is less than half full and the balance in my bank account is seventy-six cents. Thankfully, I work from home and don't have to deal with the horrors of not having enough gas to make it to work for the rest of the week. I only move my car on Tuesday for choir practice, Thursday for dance and Bible Study, Saturday for dance, and Sunday for church.

I am a single mother in every aspect of the word. I'm not married and never have been. I am not dating nor do I have any prospects. My daughter is eleven years old and very unhappy about being an only child. Her dad lives several states away and she is not very happy that he is now trying to be a part of her life. She asked if she could have a brother or sister. I told her that she has three younger siblings from her dad. She says, "They're not from you so that doesn't count."

My dear darling daughter is always my entertainment. Some days, I think she is oblivious to the fact that we don't have money for certain things. Just today, when she came home from school, she asked her favorite question, "What's for dinner?"

Because I am still at work when she comes home, I answer with a raised finger to say, "Just a minute," as I try to finish the call that I happen to be on. She puts her things down and comes back to wait for my answer. I give her the day's dinner menu.

Her reply is, "Is there anything else?"

It's those moments I want to pack her up and take her either to my mom or to her dad and walk away. Some days, I don't eat until dinner as that's all the food we have in the house. She eats breakfast and lunch at school because paying for a month's worth of reduced lunch will feed her more than using that same amount of money to buy groceries.

Now, before you get started on why I don't reach out for some help, let me give you this. I am currently working full time at a "good job" for the state. This job is about $1,100/month less than what I used to make when I was a teacher.

When I lost my job as a teacher, I had to file Chapter 13 in order to survive. When I sat in the office with the lawyer and he looked at my budget and said, "I hate to insult you and I hope you don't take this the wrong way, but how do two people survive off of $119 a month for groceries?"

I replied, "We manage. I've learned to shop the sales and do my darnedest to use coupons."

"Have you considered applying for Food Stamps?" he asked.

Up until that moment, I had been in tears because he had just informed me that my bankruptcy might not be approved because my budget was so tight. When I heard this question, I burst into hysterical laughter.

"I determine eligibility for other people for that program. I am paid just enough so that I am not eligible."

At this point, I'm sure he didn't know if I was sane, or about to jump through the window. That was it for his questions for me.

I gave up my fancy smartphone for a prepaid service. My child does not have a cell phone (she doesn't need one!) and we don't have cable. We do have Internet and that is how we watch television. The only reason we have Internet right now though, is because it is required for my job. My budget is very tight, but we manage by God's grace.

Most of my daughter's friends have cell phones with all the bells and whistles. They all also have social media accounts. She is dying to get a page, but I told her that she is too young and it is something we'll reassess when she gets older. She pouts and tries to beg. When I say that's the end of it, she storms into her room and doesn't want to talk to me for the rest of the day. I don't press her. I know she is a preteen and this is how they behave. So, I let her have her moments.

When I get depressed, I try not to let her know, but she can feel it. It's those days that she will come sit at my feet or on my lap (yes, with her eleven-year-old self, she comes to sit in my lap). Now that she is in middle school, it is not "cool" to be seen with me, so in the morning when she goes to the bus stop and I am going for my morning walk, she walks ahead of me. She knows good and well if anybody sees us, they will know I am her mom! Just this last Saturday, she was in a parade here in town. The man sitting next to me tapped me as she was coming up and said, "That's your daughter right there, huh?" It's always obvious. We look so much alike.

Some days, when I look at her, I remember the early years when she completely and totally depended on me for everything. Now, she's a big girl and is making her mom proud. She is so very independent. She makes plans for her future and is not afraid to dream big.

On the days when she makes me angry for being seemingly ungrateful or irresponsible with something that I fought hard to pay for, I try to remember her progress from childhood to adolescence. I think of all the days that she has encouraged me to do what it takes to be a better me. It is then that I know I will do whatever I can to make sure she has everything she needs and as much of what she wants that will let her be a good person.

I know I talk a lot about struggling, but I am grateful for my struggle. Knowing that God is in charge and provides for my needs has helped me understand that I am really not in charge of anything. My job is to do everything I can to please Him. That includes doing the best I can to take care of the gift of my daughter, so that is what I will do. If that means I have to go down the street and get a job sewing buttons on people's fingernails to make ends meet, then I will. I think it has made me a stronger person and has given me a chance to really get to know God and appreciate my role as a mother. While my daughter is going through her phases of adolescence, I am taking cues from Him on how to deal and how to keep pressing. She will be awesome, despite our current situation. I know that God has a plan and that my latter days will be better than my former.

Kimyatta Walker is a mom of one child who has entered those preteen/ adolescent years. Kimyatta likes to read, sing, and listen to music. Currently, she lives in Villa Rica, GA and is awaiting the perfect time for life's next adventure.

Diary of a Mom With a ~~Big Heart~~ Disability
BY MIRANDA PARKER

The moment my daughter first looked at me, my life made sense.

We were in a periwinkle labor and delivery room at DeKalb Medical Center in East Atlanta, Georgia. My best friend coached me through Lamaze and natural childbirth. It took only six hours, but the process took a lot from me. My body had been screaming for rest before my water broke. I was beyond exhausted. I didn't know what death felt like, but I was deathly tired.

Yet, my daughter's big, brown eyes and baby doll eyelashes staring back at me brought me back to life. It was like she spoke to my soul and blessed it. God moved through her to me. Glorious. For one of the most important moments in my life the reality that God existed, that He knew me, and that becoming a mom to her was a part of His plan for me ignited passion, power, and this strong will for me to give her the best life possible.

For that moment, I believed I could do anything. And then our future vanished before the sound of my daughter's first coo.

While the nurses bathed and tagged her feet, I was in the process of dying.

THE BOTTOM FALLS OUT AND IT AIN'T DIAPERS.

After nine months (baby was a preemie) of eating fresh fruit and vegetables, walking, enduring heartburn that would choke a hairy cat, and reminding our daughter's father that he would pay dearly for putting me through this and missing her birth, I was dying. It took another ten months to confirm that I was terminal.

Peripartum Pulmonary Hypertension. One year left to live—tops. I was devastated.

My ex was so devastated that he…well, the "ex" part gave it away. He left me in the hospital when my skin began turning gray and I had been placed on the heart transplant waiting list. His reason for abandoning me and our daughter was that he felt guilty.

Don't hate him. Apparently 21 percent of men dip on their dying spouses[1], so…It was all good in my hood. During that time, my main focus was making sure that my daughter was surrounded by the people who would be there for her forever. So his departure made it easy for me to know who would be there for her when I left. And who wouldn't break her heart later.

Now that I knew who would parent her when I left, I began writing a diary to her. I wanted her to know who I was and I wanted to offer her some advice as she approached certain milestones in her life.

The more I wrote, the more other people asked me to write for them. While attending a relative's funeral, a newspaper founder offered me a gig to write for the paper. He knew I was dying and knew I didn't want to sit around waiting for it. I didn't and so I accepted his offer.

And then something unbelievable happened.

MIRACLES SWOOP LIKE BOOMERANGS.

A cardiologist, whom I tutored in high school, saw me in ICU and reviewed my chart. He had just studied a disease that had

1 Glantz, M. J., Chamberlain, M. C., Liu, Q., Hsieh, C.-C., Edwards, K. R., Van Horn, A. and Recht, L. (2009), Gender disparity in the rate of partner abandonment in patients with serious medical illness. Cancer, 115: 5237–5242. doi: 10.1002/cncr.24577.

similar symptoms to mine. This disease had a better prognosis. He life-flighted me to Emory Hospital, where two doctors, specializing in Peripartum Cardiomyopathy saved my life.

I was going to live, y'all.

Believe me, if I could have jumped, I would have, but I couldn't. Because although I got to live, now I had to live with one of the hardest diseases to manage, while taking care of an infant without her very fit father.

At the time, I was a project manager for an architect firm, very proficient to the point of ad nauseum. I planned for a living. Moreover, I was a bibliophile. Everything I needed until that point could be found in a book, journal, or magazine. I promise you…I found nothing.

What was I going to do? How could I raise a well-adjusted child while operating a wheelchair, breathing with an oxygen tank, and being heavily medicated?

So I tried my best and found myself back into the hospital again. I needed physical and occupational therapy. Again, because I had no book or source material on how to live with this disease, I wasn't aware that people with chronic illnesses have to relearn how to walk, breathe, basic activities we take for granted.

This time, my family began to talk among themselves about how to take care of my daughter, while I completed therapy. My grandmom had a stroke and my mom was taking care of her, so she couldn't.

My dad, a retired U.S. Marine, who hadn't been around small children in twenty years stepped up as Super Granddad. He received a lot of help from his new wife, a retired nurse, and my aunt.

I felt at peace about my daughter being taken care of, but I had a huge amount of fear of never being able to be a parent on my own. The fear disabled me further.

WHO STOLE DAD'S CAR?

It took watching the Twin Towers collapse on television September 11, 2001, for me to regain my fire to parent my daughter. There was something about the finality and the horror in what happened to innocent people. A voice so clear to me whispered in my ear, "You are among the living, so live."

I got out my chair, took my dad's car keys, and went to see about my baby at my aunt's house. Although I was scared to do it, I moved away from my dad and aunts, so that I could put my big girl panties on and parent this child despite my disability. My family had been very good to me, but if I was going to be who I wanted to be—who God told me I was when my daughter first looked at me, I had to be that person now. If nothing else, the tragedy of 9/11 taught me that I need to fight fear and live.

As my child grew into her toddler season, I got better, stronger, out of the wheelchair, off the oxygen, and into pretty good shape for a woman with a weak heart.

Twelve years later, I am the proud parent of a Bronze Award Girl Scout (aiming for her Silver), all-A student in the gifted program, Honors Band clarinet player and softball player, who is the sweetest soul I have ever met. Her teachers love her. Her friends' parents love her. She is lovely.

When I think about all she is as an upcoming teenager, my heart bubbles with so much love and awe and thanksgiving for this girl. I cannot believe she is my daughter. I cannot believe who I am now because of this girl.

Guess my dad needs his car back…

THREE TRUTHS, BUT NOT IN THIS ORDER

Because of my disability, I couldn't return to work. My Social Security disability check provides our basic needs, while my contract as a published author with a New York publishing house gives us the cushion to have a great Christmas, to get all my daughter's school supplies, go to the movies, not live hand to mouth. I'm an author. Can you believe that?

I am also spokesperson for the American Heart Association's Go Red for Women Campaign. CNN featured my story in 2012[2] and I continue to work for the advancement of mothers with heart challenges.

Also, since I couldn't find the information I needed about being a disabled parent, I am writing a series of how-to-parent guides for moms with disabilities that I plan to launch in 2013. Being a mom with disabilities has many challenges. Here are some tips I learned along the way that helped me this far:

1. HAVE A FAMILY ACTION PLAN FOR WHEN THE ILLNESS TAKES OVER.

Sometimes no matter what you do, the illness desires her time to come out of her castle. So I have a team of family members, friends, schoolteachers, Girl Scout leaders, my doctors, and my daughter's pediatrician who know what to do for her when I can't do.

This year, for instance, I had a lupus flare. (The source of my heart failure was undiagnosed, pregnancy-induced lupus.) Last year was stressful for me and I forgot to close the drawbridge to the castle where the Lupus Dragon lives inside of me. So she woke up and wreaked all kinds of havoc in my body. My heart, my lungs, my nervous system, and my blood were all attacked. For almost a year, while trying to write and promote my novels,

---

2 Survivor of heart failure dedicates birthday to educating other women
http://www.cnn.com/2012/01/30/us/iyw-stewart-go-red/index.html

as well as prepare my child for middle school, I had to endure some of the sickest and most painful days of my life. Had I not had a support team in place, my daughter also would have suffered.

2. FROM JUMP STREET, SET YOUR PLACE AS THE HEAD OF YOUR CHILD'S CLASSROOM

Your child's teacher, God bless him or her, doesn't have a clue about life as a disabled parent. He or she will send out these notes to parents to do things that are impossible for you to do (field trip volunteer, field day volunteer, helping your child build a rocket, etc.). Instead of sharing your story of why you physically can't do it, tell them at "Meet the Teacher Day" who you are and explain what they are going to do in their role as your teaching assistant for the year.

Some clear communication rules need to apply. And you have to be adamant about these rules, because sometimes you can't come to curriculum night. Sometimes you're in the hospital and your kid needs your signature for something important and you can't sign it, but you can email your child's teacher from your phone. You can have pinch-hitter parents from your team step in for you. There are options. If you present those options at the beginning of the school year, then you control the environment needed to continue parenting your child.

However, if you give the teachers your rules and they don't like them, then give them an ultimatum that if they can't adhere to these rules, the school administration will move your child out of that class. I have done that only once and since then, a universe of open communication has showered me. See. Teachers and principals talk. They talk about the parent who won't take no for an answer. Me. Now I know everything about what happens in my daughter's class. I am privy to information before the entire class at times. I have been PTA Vice President, Parent Rep for the School Council and even head of Pre-K and Head Start for my daughter's county school system by being my child's chief teacher.

3. DATING AND BEING DISABLED WITH A CHILD.

Honey, I stopped dating, but I met a great guy, while in the hospital. I had to have a blood transfusion. This tall man came into my room wearing scrubs and carrying a kit to administer a painful medical procedure. I immediately began to cry. To my chagrin, he was a respiratory therapist who had come into the wrong room. He was so touched by the fear in my eyes that he offered to come back during his lunch and read the Bible for me. Really? We have been together since. He is a father who had custody of his now grown daughters, and he loves my kid like his own. (Has her on his life insurance policy and everything). My advice? If you can meet a man who works in health care, then befriend him, love him, and cherish him. It saves you on having to explain your illness. He's not surprised when you get sick in front of him and he won't run away when you do. Plus, he can even help you when you're in distress.

I could tell you stories about me and other men that would crack you up...and break your heart. But at the end of the day, you need a guy with a built-in tolerance for illness and parenthood. Period. I'm trying to save your heart here.

As my daughter enters the world of Teenagedom, y'all pray for us. Pray for her. Now more than ever, I believe in the life God gave me. I'm not bitter about experiencing almost every day of her life, something many working parents aren't able to do. I'm not bitter about her dad, allowing me to meet a great, great man who fits into our lives like comfy, worn slippers. I'm not bitter about having this enlarged heart, because it is big and wide enough to take it all in. And it's made me brave enough to fight the dragons inside of me on nights when I could easily have given up.

Don't you give up. Allow your life to make sense.

Sadly, only weeks after penning this entry, Miranda Parker lost her battle with heart disease. She will be remembered by her family, friends, literary colleagues, and all the lives she touched through the written word. Find out more about her at www.mirandaparker.com

Printed in the United States
By Bookmasters